the way into faerie

RAE BETH

ROBERT HALE

First published in 2017 by Robert Hale, an imprint of The Crowood Press Ltd, Ramsbury, Marlborough, Wiltshire SN8 2HR

www. crowood.com

www.halebooks.com

British Library Cataloguing-in-Publication Data
A catalogue record for this book is available from the British Library.

ISBN 978 0 7198 1356 6

Disclaimer
This book contains some references to herbs that may be used to increase psychic awareness. I cannot recommend that these should be taken if you are also taking prescribed medicines (or even some over-the-counter ones). In fact, it is now against the law for anyone except a doctor to advise that you should. Please ask your doctor for advice if you are confused about this. Meanwhile, don't let it put you off pursuing a fey path. The ingesting of herbs is not an essential part of it, anyway.

Typeset by Derek Doyle & Associates, Shaw Heath
Printed and bound in India by Replika Press Pvt Ltd

CONTENTS

This book is dedicated to
my beloved, inspiringly fey,
generous-spirited mother

ELIZABETH ELLEN
(known sometimes as 'Betty')

1929–2016

Author's Note

This book is not scholarly but experiential, as it is my belief that that which relates to what we call the Otherworld can touch our hearts, and this is its true value. However, I must explain my usage of some of the words that will appear in this book as today, there is no real consensus about them.

I have regularly used the words 'fey', 'fae' and 'fay' with these meanings.

fey   A person with psychic and mystical sensitivity or abilities.

fae   One of the faerie kind. Note that I have also used the word elf to mean this, because the Anglo-Saxons used the term elf generically – much as we now use the later, Latin-derived term 'faerie' to mean 'a spirit perceived in Nature'.

Fay   An enchantress or enchanter.

Sometimes, I have used what may be confusing punctuation. For example, the word 'faerie' spelt with a small 'f' refers to one of the Fae. With a capital 'F', it means a place – the Otherworld.

'Nature' is spelt with a capital 'N' even when in mid-sentence because I am using it to denote 'all-there-is' in both this and the Otherworld, including spirits of the dead and faeries. As will become clear, I do not believe anything is outside or beyond some aspect or another of natural processes. However, there is nothing reductionist in what follows as I am very sure that there is another order of reality as valid as this in which we live, peopled by 'otherkind' as well as by the dead. In which belief, I join with those following indigenous traditions throughout the Ages and throughout the World as well as with those of any religion at all (or none) who sense this other order of being *within* rather than outside natural existence, wild places, Nature.

Rae Beth
West of England, 2016

CHAPTER ONE

ON BEING FEY

I am a fey type, myself. I know that I am supposed to apologize for that – as though such unworldliness were forever and always a very bad thing, and bound to lead to terrible slipshod thinking or some kind of weirdness. I have to tell you that I feel passionate about correcting this impression. True, some of us can fall into a state of whimsicality, but there are a great many more of us who are both fey and unsentimental. Here is just one example of what it can be like.

Mrs Eldridge, a fey woman, leans out from her bedroom window one evening and looks at the moonlit garden, which is graced by an apple tree, not now in leaf. She hears an owl cry and she watches a star. She senses that her Otherworldly kin are very near and yet much too far away, and that the everyday World that we live in can be all too alienating. (Well, think of all those news broadcasts that are inaccurate, to say the least; and how there is too much brutality in the World; and how so much is done in a bureaucratic way that is inefficient and inhuman.)

Mrs Eldridge struggles with the complexity of the simplistic life we are now being encouraged to lead. When she wants something like a book – Mrs Eldridge is very fond of books – she whistles like a thrush and then she speaks a short rhyme. And she knows that, as a result, very soon the book will appear in a local shop or else be loaned to her with no further trouble. Yes, she knows that she can easily and cheaply order the book online, but she prefers to live in a World with proper bookshops. She also knows that any spell she casts may shape her life in ways that are not immediately obvious, for good or ill. For that which lives in the light must cast a shadow. And a gain must be balanced by a giving. (It is because she is so Otherworldly that she has become nobody's fool.)

'Oh, this human life,' she thinks now. 'So many people as predatory as any owl or shark, yet far less innocent. And oh, these endless newspapers and screens busily withholding information while trying to tell us all what we *should* believe.'

Mrs Eldridge bids her fey spirit to unfold. She bids it to prevail throughout her life, with its feet like those of a heron or swan and its wings like willow swaying in the wind. This is a spirit aware of itself as a part of the natural World, and yet it is a human spirit as much as is the more conventional kind. But sometimes she fears that there is not enough strength in it; not enough to withstand all that passes here for normality.

'Be what you really are,' the elves whisper to her. 'Therein lays your power. Reach out in spirit to all kindred spirits – therein lies survival (your spirit unbroken). Tend to your own hearth and cast your spells to heal and to bless – therein lies success.'

'Just whistle like a bird and speak a magical rhyme? And use enchantment for good, knowing I am supported in spirit by other fey people?' asks Mrs Eldridge.

'Just be in communion with us. If you ask the elves to

bear witness to your spells, that will be enough to make your spells effective and to bring help from the Otherworld. Just sing like a bird inside your soul, unheard by any human ears, and speak a spell while you wave your wand. This has always worked before. Why doubt it now? Why doubt the strength of spirit that is in Nature?

'Just imagine silver shoes on your feet, hidden by the brown boots you wear over them, and know that you walk in two Worlds at one and the same time: the Otherworld and the everyday World of living humanity.'

'Who am I,' asks Mrs Eldridge, 'that I should be as strong as you say and yet so incongruously placed? There are others like me, other fey people; I am not alone. But we often feel overwhelmed by the clamour of hectic life. Remind me – what are we doing here? And what *is* this realm of ruthlessness, insanity and greed? I mean, tell me why are we here?'

Oh, that heart-rending question! It must have been asked in the Dark Ages and beyond then in old Atlantis, and at times and in places that no one now has ever heard of. Perhaps it is eternal.

'Sing, Mrs Eldridge! Chant and bespell in your own way. Help to make all more well. Perhaps you will find an answer. But don't get too distracted by too many human anxieties. Look up at the stars. We are all – humankind, elves, trees, planets, seas, all creatures – made out of starfire. We are all one. In this knowledge, the healing spell for your World is truly begun. So chant your spells for healing and peace. You are a long way from understanding the heart of all human Mysteries; or the true worth of this often noble, crass, violent, caring, insane and creative dominant species. But you know enough to bespell for good, and so to do your best. And so let all worries cease. Winter is always followed by spring, however long that winter season. (Sometimes, it may take many thousands of years.) The song of the lark is eventually heard in the sky instead of owl-cry or the moan of the wind, or the cries of dying soldiers, or silences.'

Like Mrs Eldridge, I have often felt as if there were another order of reality to which I belong rather more than to this one. Somewhere both beautiful and strange and yet entirely familiar. And how I long for it!

To say that there is such a place is to invite ridicule. And yet the folk traditions of lands all over the World, along with shamanic teachings, do tell us so. Here in Britain, it has been called *Annwn*, *Elphame*, 'the Land Behind the North Wind', and many other names: to the Irish, it is *Tír na nÓg*, 'the Land of the Ever Young', or *Tir Tairngiri*, *Tir na Sorcha*, *Mag Mell* or *Hy-Brasil*; to the Norse, it was Faroe ('Faerie') or 'the Land of the Hella cunni'; to the Germans, 'the Land at the bottom of Mother Holle's Well'.

Faerie . . . the Otherworld. The fey feel at home with this – or, at least, with the idea of it. I am speaking here of a craving for that which is spoken of in some old tales and ballads; those concerned with life and death, blood and snow-light, sun in a forest glade, meetings with dwarves, a boat made of glass, a horse bearing fifty silver bells plaited into his mane, shape-shifting, enchantment. It is an entirely natural place and our ancestors felt that this is where the dead go. You might call it 'the Soul of Nature'. But what has it got to do with being a fey type?

The Scots used to call people *fey* if they could see or sense spirits or hear spirit messages. According to the Oxford English Dictionary, the term fey means 'fated to die'. Therefore, someone close enough to the Otherworld to see visions, meet spiritual presences, and perhaps to foretell the future. Well, we are all fated to die, eventually. And so does this mean that there is a bit of the fey in each of us, however hidden? Yes, I do think so; and it does *not* depend upon being close to death. (I have, myself, been fey since I was a small child and I am now in my sixties.) But many people stamp on this feeling within themselves; they suppress it, ignore it. Perhaps they fear being seen as cranky, or perhaps they cannot find the time for something they fear might undermine their ability to be practical. But if, reader, you are of the type to whom a gentle psychic awareness seems both natural and enriching, then the fey in you is not clamped down. It is awake and alive and active, even if in quite small and seemingly undramatic ways, such as the ability to sense when a friend is going to phone you or visit. Or the fact that you can always feel the psychic atmosphere in any house whether or not there are people living there. This is not because you are close to death – you may be a long way from that – but because you are closer than most to Otherworldly reality and do not actually see that as somehow opposed to this World. Your life includes the liminal dimension as well as the everyday and the mundane. You sense, and you may see or hear, Otherworldly reality, but you do love life. In spite of all the horror and the banality reflected in newspapers and on the internet – and in spite of the insanity of damage caused to the environment – you may be passionate about this living World. Here. In fact, in my experience, most fey people are very involved with life and are often enthusiastic about their latest creative project or career move or romance. We do not tend to become cynical.

However, we who are fey may not find this World's reality at its most shallow at all comfortable. And our perspective and skills may not always be easy for other people to understand. Still, there are a surprisingly large number of us and most of us feel that we are here for a purpose that can make sense of our struggle.

If we bravely explore the threshold area between this

and the Otherworld, and even explore the Otherworld itself – at least in our dreams and visions – we may then more easily see what that purpose is. We may also develop our own fey abilities and knowledge in the process.

Fey people have always existed. In earlier cultures many of us would have been respected as wisewomen, cunning men, shamanic healers or seers. Some have been able to see or sense angels. (The poet William Blake did this.) Many have been inspired as artists by seeing the numinous within Nature. Others have sometimes heard voices of the dead or have seen them as apparitions or else in visions. Nowadays, many who do conventional and even arduous mainstream jobs have an awareness of spirit presences and a sense of being guided. Most are highly sensitive to the spirit of place.

Historically, none of this was connected with any particular set of beliefs, and nor is it now. Back then (in Britain and throughout Europe), a fey person could be a Pagan or a Christian. Nowadays, they could be one of these or a 'New Ager'; they could be a Buddhist, Hindu, Muslim, Spiritualist – even agnostic. Being fey is about how you are made rather than about your brand of beliefs. Though, of course, some forms of spirituality – principally Paganism and Spiritualism – have supported fey people while other belief systems often have not.

In Britain today, the spirituality of a fey person may be quite anarchic and entirely private and have no basis in any organized religion. So it can be a secret spirituality that informs the fey type and this may be largely experiential. It has often been perceived as a threat by people who like ideas (and other people) to be tied down and under control and by the organizations that such people have created.

Meanwhile, in much of today's World, fey people (and those hidden bits of the fey in everybody) have been thoroughly marginalized.

So I write this book after mustering my courage and my defiance to suggest ways in which we might understand Otherworldly realities without abandoning common sense or congratulating ourselves that we belong to a special group. And to suggest ways in which we can understand how our perceptions and psychic skills can serve life.

In Britain, mainstream opinion in these reductionist times is quite adamant that there is no Otherworld to understand (no place you could see or walk around in, anyway). There may be other dimensions, as quantum physicists have told us, but these have nothing to do with anything psychic. And your state of mind and your type of awareness have no effect upon your physical reality (in spite of Schroedinger's famous cat). Neither the living nor the dead can pass into any other dimension of Nature than this one here.

Yet opinion is still divided about what we might expect after death. On the one hand, there is the materialist position I have just described. In this, there is no Otherworld in any sense in which the term has been used in folklore, indigenous tradition or spirituality. Nature is here and now and that is it and all about it. On the other hand, there are ideas based on religious teachings that include the expectation of a Heaven (and sometimes also a Hell) located somewhere *outside* Nature. In such systems, it can be acceptable to see angels since they are mentioned in the Bible and in the books of mainstream faiths other than Christianity. But it is not acceptable to see faeries, who are known to be very much linked with Nature, nor to believe that Nature is the realm of soul and spirit as well as body.

Nowadays, faeries and their realm are thought to be make-believe, anyway. Yet to people of earlier centuries, they were as real and chancy as a wild swan or a sudden gust of wind or a swooping owl. And the word *faerie* still glimmers with natural magic, rather like a mistle thrush that sings at the calm centre of a storm and yet is of that swirling wind and rain and the silver light that flashes through it. It is precisely that which can make it seem unacceptable – the fact that the Otherworld of Faerie is recognized as an aspect of Nature. For any acceptable idea of the Otherworld must transcend Nature – or so we have been somehow led to believe.

However, I have met many Christians whose beliefs are not about a Heaven and Hell filled only with humans and angels or demons and somehow beyond Nature. And my own ideas about the sacredness of both Nature and evolution were once helped along by a writer called Teilhard de Chardin, who was a Christian monk and a scientist. It is not so much religion or science that pose problems for the acceptability of fey ideas. It is, instead, the embracing of stereotypes and dogma. And this can be found amongst people of any religious belief, or, indeed, of none.

All through the Ages, there have been people who were involved with a palpable, knowable Otherworld in some way. Some were shamanic healers, seers, priestesses or priests, hedge witches or Druids. These and other groups had a framework of traditional knowledge still in use today. Also, there were and are individuals who belonged to none of these groups, but who somehow 'just knew' about Other reality. Myself, I seem to belong in both categories. So come with me and I will introduce you to the Otherworld and to some who live therein with this 'Rough Guide to Faerie'. We will see how easy, and also how healing, it can be to relate to the Otherworld while we are alive and fully committed to doing our best in this World's reality.

CHAPTER TWO

VARIOUS PORTALS

We are all walking to the Otherworld throughout our lives. However long we live, we will be there when we have died so our walk through life is taking us there. Rationality tells us that this is the only way we can ever enter the Otherworld. But throughout history there have been people who have been back and forth between this and the Otherworld while alive – or claimed that they did. Most of these journeys were undertaken only in spirit. That is to say, the person concerned would have been in some kind of trance in which they were able to explore the Otherworld psychically rather than physically. But our folklore in Britain and the evidence from some witch trials by the Inquisition suggest that there have been exceptions to this. Also, there is the written account by the seventeenth-century Reverend Robert Kirk, a minister of the Scottish Church, describing the Otherworld and its inhabitants.

Robert Kirk is believed to have entered the Otherworld while living. Eventually, he was forced to stay there rather than dying here in the more usual manner – or so his legend tells. In the nineteenth century, the folklorist W.Y.

Evans-Wentz collected other stories of physical journeys into the Otherworld by the living, including some about alleged abductions of human beings by faerie folk. These are recorded in his book, *The Fairy Faith in Celtic Countries*, first published by Oxford University Press in 1911.

Many people from lands all over the World have talked about straying or being led into some other World or dimension than that we live in here. Often, their stories have been disparaged or ignored, yet it has always been said that there are places and times in which a portal can appear (a 'portal' being an opening between this and the Otherworld). Perhaps these claims would not sound so outrageous if we ceased to think of the Otherworld as a supernatural place. For what is meant by this word 'supernatural'? My dictionary explains that it means 'above the forces of Nature' or 'beyond what Nature will account for'. But the animism that underlies traditional belief in Faerie does not necessarily imply any such thing. Another or parallel dimension does not have to be outside or beyond Nature in any way; it is simply another aspect – like the other face of the coin, perhaps, or the dark side of the Moon. In this Age of quantum physics, it may be easier than it was to accept this idea. However, in invoking Science, I am not suggesting any reductionist approach. The Otherworld is natural, yes, but Nature is profound in spirit, is magical and is of Mystery, even when (as in this World) we understand how things work and know about physics.

Be that as it may, the commonest route taken by the living into the Otherworld has always been the spirit journey, undergone in an 'altered state'. Shamanic cultures around the World have probably always used hallucinogenic herbs for this.

In Britain, many traditional witches, inheritors of our own indigenous magical techniques, once used herbs such as aconite and belladonna to facilitate a spirit flight to the Otherworld. This kind of journey does not necessarily have to be undertaken while under the influence of hallucinogenic herbs: it can be brought about by psychic work on its own. But taking hallucinogens has always had a great appeal and has often been part of rites that were held to be both important and sacred. However, it is as well to remember that aconite and belladonna are poisonous. It is now thought that very small but gradually increasing doses may have been taken by people in the past in order to build up a tolerance. But how small were the doses and how frequent? We no longer know. What we do know is that mistakes with these herbs can cause paralysis and even death.

There are less dangerous substances that have been used in Britain. These include the fungi known popularly as 'magic mushrooms' (which are now illegal and can earn you a prison sentence!) and other plants, which may or may not be reasonably safe. I am not knowledgeable about any of these plants, whether from Britain or elsewhere, because hallucinogens have never seemed to me to be the answer. Like many fey people, I find that I do not need them. Anyway, I have always been very keen to find out how far you could go without any substances to force open the inner doors. What I do like to use occasionally are the more *gentle* herbs.

There are safe ways to take herbs for psychic development. Herbal teas (such as willow, dandelion, eyebright or vervain) can gently boost your fey abilities. A strong tea of borage is said to be very effective. Thyme is a herb traditionally said to help you see faeries, whether you carry a sprig in your pocket or drink it as a tea. Mugwort is believed to help with any psychic work, including the taking of spirit journeys or the seeing of spirits in magic mirrors or crystal balls. Elder can assist in speaking with loved ones amongst the dead and with seeing faerie folk.

Such herbs are mild and may grow in your garden or can be bought from a herbal supplier. You can also buy herbs from other lands than your own, but it is said to be best, on the Faerie path, to use those that have been grown in the land where you are actually living. As far as I know, every land on Earth produces some herbs that can boost psychic awareness, but one of the first rules of working with Faerie is that we need a strong physical connection with the area in which we are trying to make a psychic link. That is, we need to eat at least some food that has been grown in that area and to drink its water and walk its pathways, become physically attuned to it in any way that we can, if we wish to sense or to see its faerie presences. 'Locally sourced' is best psychically as well as environmentally, it would seem!

Such herbs as thyme and borage are not hallucinogens, of course, but we may still need to take care. So it is up to anyone of us to make sure that we have no medical contra-indications for anything that we might want to use, even as a tea. Some herbs are bad for pregnant women and others may be dangerous if you have particular ailments or are taking prescribed medicine.

Apart from these cautions, herbal teas are easy to make and gentle on your body. They will not cause you to lose awareness of everyday reality. Their use is in a more long-term and gradual growth of psychic skills.

Do bear in mind that you may want to walk cautiously towards psychic experience. It is one thing to exchange messages of love with your dead friends or family members and to hear guidance from a wise faerie being. It is quite another to have awareness of all kinds of spirits all day, wherever you are. I have known people who have found that the Otherworld became all too overwhelming for them, and they have had to step back and focus on something like academic study or a practical task. So it is really very important to take matters at your own pace.

Actually, dramatic experiences are not the point. They can be awesome and life-changing in a constructive way. But they are not what fey abilities are actually for. These have many other uses – magical and psychic – which can bring an enhancement of life and . . . well, a healing of hearts, our own and others'. We are shown something of the Mysteries of Other reality and of life and death. We glimpse the very real connections between the Otherworld and this, and it is a healing awareness we can share. And there is more than that. According to my faerie spirit guide – my faerie teacher – we help to hold a certain psychic territory on behalf of the human race. It is the liminal state 'between the Worlds', the state in which we live in awareness of the wild magic in Nature and the spirit presences therein, that we can know as the Worlds merge and mingle inside ourselves. Without this flame of consciousness, a dim and wavering though it must sometimes seem, the whole psyche of humankind as a species could be much bleaker than people realize; for we do not represent dogma or superstition, but rather, an openness to Mystery all around us within Nature.

This is not in opposition to scientific exploration any more than poetry is in opposition to a study of grammar. It is precisely because it is so difficult to define, that a fey experience can be such a healing thing. It is not fixed, but forever questing and informal and personal – a natural mysticism that allows us to call our souls our own; a faerie spirituality rather than a religion – but what is that like in practice, you may wonder?

Sunday 12 October 2014

Today, my companions in Faerie and their World seem much further away than usual. This is because I am numb with the usual human anxieties: money, domestic problems, housing – the usual. But then I see that the ragged October winds are bringing down leaves; translucent grey skies are shaded with darker grey; and the rushing clouds and dying autumnal flowers all tell of the thinning of veils between this and the Otherworld – which always heralds winter. In spite of my preoccupations, I go out into the garden. I can sense Faerie gates beginning to open. They are not pretty: beautiful and awe-inspiring, the winter gates – storm-grey and silver and pearl and dark shades of purple – very different from the summer gates, which are equally as beautiful, but not at all sombre.

The powers that open the gates between this World and the Other are as strong as those that bring the waves of the Atlantic pounding onto the west coast of Britain, or set the stars to rise in the evening sky. There is nothing I can do or need to do about any of this. I see and sense the gates and am comforted by their implacability. As the year dies, the beloved Dead and the hosts of Faerie come closer whether we acknowledge them or not.

I go back indoors and light a candle on my writing desk, saying, 'I light this to my ancestors, all my dead forebears, those men and women of my whole family tree. Wherever they are now, whether within the Otherworld or reborn within this one, may they all be blessed with good health of spirit, soul and body.'

My faerie teacher now speaks to me within my mind. She comments that I also have ancestors of spirit, meaning all those men and women who have inspired and taught me, and so have helped to make me what I am. And I should not forget my most distant forebears, whose lives preceded the human race, the ancestors of other races than human, who have made human lives possible by their own part in evolution; nor should I forget the land itself; the actual area where I live, which has ancestors ('landcestors'), creatures (including human, plant and mineral) who have made it what it is. And Mother Earth, the planet by which we all have been given birth – the Ancestress of all. And the Great Mother–Father, the Source, meaning whatever Powers of Nature began every course of the stars in the Universe and all existence in this and the Otherworld.

Truly, I am descended from that which is Ancestress–Ancestor of All. I am kin to the plants and creatures and one with each life that has ever been lived. As are we all.

I say, 'May this flame burn within the Otherworld as it burns here. I offer it particularly to my Dad and my grandparents and to my faerie familiars and teachers as a token of love and gratitude. May I be guided by them in love and wisdom. We are all of one fire, one Spirit, wherever we are. And so can never be sundered, but instead be changed in our ways and connections.'

Through my own ancestors, I can reach back to the Source of All and so know myself at one with every being, at least in spirit (if not in mind or soul or attitude). In spirit, where we are each innocent (if not wise), for spirit is pattern, energy, archetype and existence, while soul/psyche may be innocent or corrupt, of goodwill or ill will, or may even attain to wisdom and full individuation. Then, moving forward in time (again, within my imagination), I renew my links with those ancestors I knew personally before they died and with my faerie familiars. I am centred now within my own being as this person I am with these particular links with the Otherworld. From the personal to the transpersonal and back again, reconnected in terms of heart and soul, here and now restored.

And so back to the washing and cleaning, the phone calls, and so on. But I feel better now that the Worlds are merged within me again.

By now, reader, you may be wondering 'What is a faerie familiar?' A familiar is simply a friend, according to my dictionary. And, according to my faerie teacher, a faerie is someone of an Otherworldly; a non-human being who dwells in the Otherworld as their natural home. Some people believe that some of the faerie races did once live in this World, but are now displaced or extinct (here). Others say that the Fae (the faeries) have never lived anywhere but the Otherworld, even though they may have a strong impact here. My faerie teacher tells me that there are species of each type in Faerie – those who have lived in our World, but who no longer do so, and those who never have. In any event, she says, they are all Otherworldly species now. There are many types, including faerie plants and creatures – an entire biosphere.

Some of the Fae have been said, in faerie lore and folklore, to have entered this World for a while. They are of warm flesh and blood and can be of more or less human appearance. Though there are said to be give-away signs (such as webbed feet, or hair with a naturally green tinge, or, amongst some men, bodies that are especially hairy). But we cannot really generalize as there are so many different types. Some are tall, smooth-skinned and beautiful, with very long fair hair; some are small and dark, and pale skinned.

There are said to be some people who have faerie ancestry as well as human. That is because there is a long tradition of human–faerie marriages. It is a theme that appears in quite a few faerie tales, such as the Welsh 'Belaney of the Lake' and the French 'Melusine'. The descendants of such marriages, being part fae, often have great ease in communing with Faerie. It is as though they have an inner portal which is ever open. This is not the great advantage you might think – or not always. It does give great sensitivity to the beauty of a landscape and to the natural magic within it. But it can also make this everyday World in which we live feel unbearably harsh and abrasive. It is best for such people to live well away from big cities and to have plenty of contact with elemental forces of Nature – wind, rain, sun, the sea or a river, or the land itself.

The most famous novel that includes human–faerie marriage is undoubtedly J.R.R. Tolkien's *Lord of the Rings*. Tolkien was steeped in Northern European faerie lore. As the Professor of Anglo-Saxon at Oxford University, he knew about early Anglo-Saxon tales and folklore as well as the Norse tradition from which they derived and the parallel Celtic mythology. (In fact, the elven woman Arwen, who marries the human Aragorn, has a name that sounds like the Welsh name Awen, so Tolkien seems to have delved into faerie lore both Celtic and Norse, with much inspiration as a result.) His own portal into the Otherworld consisted of learning as well as of imagination.

To get back to the subject of faerie familiars, if you are fey, you may have some without being consciously aware of it. For they may remember you from your time in the Otherworld before birth, even if you do not yet remember them. You may see them psychically without quite recognizing them. This is said to be especially easy at those times when the veil of unknowing between the two Worlds is thinner than usual. Traditionally, it is said that these times are the:

- dawn and dusk of every day
- nights of the New or Full Moon
- days and nights of all the old Celtic and Norse festivals, particularly Beltaine (1 May) and Samhain (31 October)

This is what is said. But in my experience, it can happen at any time. You may see faerie familiars with inner sight (that is, with your eyes closed as if waking from a dream), or you may see them physically (with your eyes open). In their own World, they would look solid; seen psychically, with eyes open in ours, they often appear as figures of white or coloured light or as a shape made of mist that is palely lit. Apparently, we look like shapes of light or mist to them, when seen psychically from their World – so it works both ways.

Some familiars may take the form of a faerie animal or bird, but these are not 'power animals' as described in some books on shamanism. Certainly, they will help to resolve problems or bring you aid if you ask for it – as power animals are said to do. But these are individual beings in their own right. Not archetypes of particular qualities but friends or, at least, companions. They may help, support and advise us if they want to but, like any friend, they may ask for our involvement with their projects, too. For example, they may ask you to sing to them for the sake of their strength while they carry out some magical task of their own in our World. Or to perform an act such as moving a stone that is blocking a path. They may have magical reasons for wanting a path in this World to be unblocked – to do with the flow of subtle energy along that route, perhaps.

Real familiars will never try to force you to do anything for yourself or for them that goes against your own moral code or which is dangerous. Indeed, they will never *force* you to do anything at all. We can reject their advice if we like. After all, we do not always do as our friends suggest in *this* World, do we? Advice from familiars is no different.

Myself, I feel that I must safeguard my own autonomy by always taking responsibility for all my own decisions. I listen to faerie advice with respect (I have found that it is usually right!), but in the end it is up to me to decide what *I* am going to do.

No spirit can ever *make* any of us do anything so long as we are in full command of ourselves. We can choose what to do. Heavy drug use or psychiatric problems can alter that situation so, of course, I do not recommend that anyone should work with Faerie unless reasonably psychologically healthy and able to be responsible for choices and actions.

Dear reader, you may not feel ready to find a familiar spirit yet, so all this may seem a bit premature. For you, it may be quite enough to sit down somewhere peaceful and talk to someone you love who has died, silently inside your mind. Tell them how very much you wish them well in the Otherworld and ask them whether there is anything they wish to say to you. There may not be an immediate answer but you may sense that in the Otherworld they have felt something, paused and remembered you. No real link of love is ever broken.

This may be painful to you if your loss has been very recent. But it can also be very healing. Small rituals can help these contacts and they can gradually become clearer. For example, you can light a candle before beginning to talk to those in Faerie, offering the light to your lost loved ones and any faerie familiars who may already be with you, And then you can ask them to help you to hear or see or sense them strongly. This kind of small rite can be fitted into a busy day. It is best if you do it regularly because then the sense of communion and connection builds up. Naturally, you should not do it in any place that has a bad psychic atmosphere or is haunted by a disturbed spirit.

You can also strengthen your links with Faerie by leaving a bowl of cream or honey on the table overnight (or anywhere pets cannot get at it) and asking them to bless you with their friendship. Such practices may not be glamorous compared to doing a complex magical rite or using hallucinogens, but they do create a kind of portal between the Worlds, an inner door – and they do it safely.

So, to recap on the subject of portals, you can find many natural openings between this World and the Otherworld, but such openings are of varying types and qualities. Traditionally, some of these can be stumbled upon accidentally. Others can be opened by psychic work or by simple rites.

First, there is that portal we all pass through at life's end – *the Gate of Death*. It is not exactly a two-way door since return can only be through the Gate of Birth and in a different life, unless we choose to return in spirit from time to time in order to visit and bless our living descendants or friends.

There are also *portals come upon accidentally*. These are portals through which we may pass while alive and that open into a part of the Otherworld – though not necessarily into that part where the dead dwell. They are natural features of the land, or appear to be so. Such portals are not usually there when we return to the same spot on another occasion. Traditionally, they can be:

- A band of mist, which lies right across a path or road and through which you walk to find yourself in another dimension.
- Two trees growing quite close together and appearing to make a natural gateway.
- An unfamiliar turning you take in a wood.
- A small decrepit-looking fence or wall that you step over.
- An unexpected opening at the back of a cave – one which does not lead into darkness but into the landscape of another place.
- A sod of earth on which you place your foot: it looks like any other part of the field, but as soon as you step onto it, you enter the Otherworld.

Needless to say, these portals are not always present and open, or everyone would know where to find them. They depend upon an interaction between your own psyche and the place and upon actions of those in the Otherworld – who may open or close such doors for special purposes. It is also possible that the reasons for an open portal may sometimes have nothing to do with the person who has inadvertently strayed through.

Then there are spirit portals, which people may find when they are spirit journeying. These have often been used by people who have taken hallucinogenic herbs meant to open the doors of consciousness. In my experience, fey people can find these doors with no herbal help by a method known as path-working, which begins as a guided visualization and then develops into something with its own volition and in which the traveller can take an active part in what is happening. This is so much easier for a person who has some experience of psychic or magical work. Going through a faerie door like this is an inner experience. It does not, of itself, lead on to a physical entry.

There are also openings which I call *'portals of the heart'* – these are my favourites. They can be created when we talk with, or bless, or in some way relate to, our ancestral kin or our faerie familiars by speaking 'from the heart'. We can speak out loud or silently, mind to mind (and heart to heart), and this may bring us into a liminal state in which we may have fleeting inner visions of those we love or hear spirit voices or sense guiding messages. We cannot only bless, but ask to be blessed. This kind of inner communion is a portal of the heart or soul. It is easily closed again by saying something like: 'Farewell for now. Thank you for this meeting. I'm going back now to the living World'. It helps if you then get up and walk around a bit to re-orientate yourself and return to everyday consciousness. (If you have no success at first with a portal of the heart, try it somewhere that is not ordinary, such as the grave of a loved one, or a quiet glade in a wood, or beside a waterfall, or anywhere you hold sacred.)

Finally, I have to say that I think an ability to find any portal into Faerie while still alive must have something to do with the path that we walk through this World. Is it a path that you would like to lead you to faerie contact, or do you feel comfortable only with the idea of human spirits? If you are fey, then you are probably happy with tree spirits, place spirits, creaturely spirits and faerie beings. Indeed, the animism that underlays all faerie lore will seem natural to you. In your mind, there will be no false division between humankind and the rest of Nature. So you will tend to walk through life seeing yourself as a part of the natural world, not apart from it.

I call the fey type of woman a 'Lizzie Webfoot'. My

name for a fey man is 'Johnnie Hoof'.

These names are not arbitrary. Lizzie, the fey, is called Webfoot partly because some faerie women are said to have webbed feet. Lizzie's own feet may or may not be slightly webbed – some people's feet are naturally – either way, she has a feeling of kinship with non-human beings of the Otherworldly kind. She also walks consciously upon the Web of Wyrd. That is the Northern European name for the great mass of connections between all beings and all places in all the Worlds. It is also the web we weave, the tapestry of our fate, created by our choices and actions and which affects others as well, just as their weavings can affect us. The Fae know all about this Web (none better!). They know it as Nature's work, with ourselves – whoever we are – as the mediums for many experimental designs throughout the Ages.

Johnnie knows about the Web, too. Not the one on the Internet (though he knows about that, obviously): the one where both magic and mundane actions reverberate; the one to which every being of every species contributes something, however short their life (even if they never know). And Johnnie's creaturely feet also denote a path of acceptance of our oneness with the rest of the natural world and of our dependence upon other species – plants, animals, minerals, the whole biosphere. And they show him to be, like Lizzie, walking a path of natural magic, however informally.

An important consequence of Lizzie Webfoot's and Johnnie Hoof's choice of path is that they try to respect the natural world in the way that they live. This means trying to do the least harm to the environment. Their fey sensitivity means that the sight of a beautiful hedgerow littered with take-away cartons people have slung out of cars causes them acute emotional pain. They are the ones likeliest to be seen leaving a beach with bags full of other peoples' empty bottles and cans which they will have removed for the sake of marine wildlife as well as for the aesthetic improvement. As far as they can afford it, they buy natural products for the home and garden. They may buy a lot of their clothes in charity shops – partly because it is cheap and fun, but also because it is an obvious way to allow clothes to be recycled. And so on.

Their webbed feet and hooves take them upon a path of rebellion against human abuses of Nature. They are not perfect about this – nobody is in today's culture – nor are they fanatical. But in a quiet way, they do care.

It is a fact that some of the Fae can become irate about any damage done to the natural world and they may act on their anger as some folklore tells us. But Lizzie and Johnnie do their best to do the least harm. This is not out of fear. It is not placatory, but is done from the heart. They would do it even if they thought that none of the Fae would notice or care. And the Fae respect that and respond with blessings.

CHAPTER THREE

Mapping the Otherworld

Maps are fascinating to me, especially Ordnance Survey maps of Somerset, where I live. But no map can really tell me what it is like to walk in Beacon Hill woods or climb Glastonbury Tor, or see a heron on the moors, flapping its angular way upwards. Maps of the Otherworld, such as they are, can do even less for us. They are more in the nature of symbols or metaphors. One of my favourites is the old Celtic idea of the 'green and flaming tree'. This conveys the belief that any tree that exists in this living World also, since all reality is multi-dimensional, exists in the Otherworld. If you look at it here, it has green leaves, in summertime, anyway. But in the Otherworld it has leaves of gold. This may be a reference to autumnal leaves since there is an old belief that in one part of Faerie the seasons are the opposite to our own. In other words, when it is spring or summer here, it is autumn or winter there (and vice versa). Perhaps it is also a way of saying that as we enter a liminal state and so prepare to enter Faerie in spirit – or even physically – we become more aware of the Earth's 'unearthliness'. And so we see that a tree is of gold – inner fire, energy, spirit – as well as solidly possessing a brown trunk and green leaves.

It is a fact that not only our own state of consciousness, but the actual resonance of our souls is crucial to any safe or life-enhancing experience of Faerie. Our whole inner state matters. This should be no surprise now that quantum physicists have explained to us that physical matter can change, physically, merely because someone pays it attention; observes it and thinks about it. So it may be important to think positively rather than fearfully about Faerie. It must also help to be entirely sincere when asking (silently, inside ourselves) for Faerie gates to open or, at least, to become visible whether or not we may pass through them. Traditionally, such requests are made 'in the name of the Faerie Queen'. And they are made to the Faerie King or to the portal keepers or guardians who serve him. These beings, as our ancestors knew them, were not the tiny, dainty creatures of some nursery tale, but powers of the Natural process of transformation, involving not just the fact of death, but the resulting changes and renewal. Faerie Queens and Kings and those who serve them are agents of alchemy – Nature's alchemy – bound up with a subtle continuum of place and fate and the interdependence of one event or being with every other.

But resonance of the soul (now that's a phrase to conjure with!) needs a bit more explanation. In all Otherworldly encounters, it is this, above all, that determines the nature of the experience. The term really means 'psychic resonance', and it is linked with 'psychic atmosphere'. In other words, it is that keynote of a person's inner being that we see manifested in their way of relating to what is around them. (Unless, of course, they are concealing their real actions and intentions, in which case their psychic resonance may be the only clue as to what is going on.) Psychic resonance is that quality which attracts people of goodwill and integrity (or not). It is that quality that makes people feel uneasy, especially fey people, if it is really bad. This resonance can be disguised by the way we dress or behave in this World, or be misread by others because of their own social, sexual or racial prejudices. But for those who *just know* if someone is to be trusted or not, it is the giveaway sign. And it is this that is the main factor in deciding whether or where we go in the Otherworld. It is far from being the only factor and it is not, in itself, simple. (Well-meaning people do not always meet with goodwill or go to nice places even in this World – reality is a lot more complex.) But our own inner resonance does play a big part. In this respect, the map of the Otherworld is inside ourselves.

It is also inside the land. This is because this World is a parallel dimension of Faerie. It sounds very strange to put it like that, but to those who live in the Otherworld, this is a parallel dimension. Either way, there are similarities and a kind of mirroring – which tends to mean that the landscapes of any area may be found in the Otherworld. However, it will not necessarily mean exact replication. For one thing, as all faerie lore tells us, 'time runs differently there'. This means that if you go through a portal in London you may not find yourself in the present-day city, but perhaps in the same location a few hundred years ago. And even then, you would not walk through the London of, say, 1816. It is well-known that those who live in the Otherworld can shift shape *and the places can alter, as well*. The laws that determine how and why this happens are natural ones. They are the laws of natural magic, and they revolve around the links between consciousness and form.

What I found when I once walked physically through a

portal in Somerset was a very lovely Somerset landscape. Not of the present day, but as it may have looked in the nineteenth century. I entered through the yard of an old disused factory that used to make furniture stuffed with horsehair. I did not know it at the time, but the business had collapsed in the 1920s. Its workshops have long since been converted and modernized and are now cottages. At the time, I merely thought I was going for a walk – exploring the edge of a small town that was then unknown to me. I had had no previous knowledge of the area. So I had no idea what it should have looked like in the twenty-first century. A few months before, I had asked my familiar spirit to help me walk right into the Otherworld and he had said that he would when the time was right. I had forgotten about it for quite a while. It certainly had not been on my mind when I had gone for that particular walk. So when he told me what was happening, I did not really believe him.

On the far side of the yard was a low barrier. It was just a thin strip of wood screwed onto a post at one end and padlocked at the other. The paint was chipped and very old. Dirty cream paint. Beyond it was a rough cart track. I stepped over.

Now I was in the most beautiful country imaginable. Fields sloped gently into a small valley on my left and then rose in folds and clefts, which held many trees. Everywhere the small fields were shaped by contours of the land and by history, and were bounded by elder, hazel, hawthorn interspersed with ash and oak and, perhaps, elm, all growing raggedly. It was that irregular and ethereal patchwork of fields fading into the haze of far-off hills that makes rural England what it is.

And not a mobile phone tower in sight! No barbed wire; no metal gates; no take-away food cartons in the hedgerow, no electric cables; and no sign of modern roads or buildings. Even now, very occasionally, you can still find such unspoilt places. So I still did not believe my familiar spirit when he said that I had just stepped through a portal.

To my left, I saw the 'barley sugar twist' chimneys of an old house surrounded by tall trees. In its grounds were slim towers built of white stone that was patterned with lichen. Later on, when researching in the town's museum, I found that there had been a mansion named Florida Place where I had walked; it was destroyed by fire in 1888. (I never did find out what the white towers could have been.)

It sounds as though I was time-travelling. And I was, in a way. For my familiar explained that in this part of the Otherworld I could walk back and back in time until I reached the twelfth century. Beyond that I could not go because no ancestors of mine were buried locally before that time. This was news to me: I had not known that any of my ancestors had been buried in that particular area. (I still have no proof that they ever were, but that is what my familiar said.)

What, you may wonder, has that got to do with it? Well, traditionally, you can only enter the ancestral aspect of the Otherworld (while living) if you are at one with the land-scape in a very particular sense – by virtue of the fact that at least one of your forebears is buried there. I do not know why this is. I only know that I had not heard of the tradition before my familiar spirit spoke about it. (A few years later, I received confirmation from the writer Orion Foxwood in his book *The Faery Teachings*.)

I did not stay long in the Otherworld; did not walk back to the twelfth century. My familiar counselled against it. He said that if I stayed and talked with those I should meet of the Otherworld, the portal would close behind me and I should not get back.

By the way, there are said to be other parts of Faerie that may be entered by the living without any ancestral connections to the place. They are, or they seem to be, those parts inhabited by the Fae rather than by humans. But I mention these ancestral links because they are very important in some cases and because this is what happened to me. It is far from being all you need to know or the only way to go. However, you may be taken by surprise one day. Most of us only know where our ancestors lived and died for a few generations back. So you could be in a region or country with which you have no known connection and yet feel that the realm of Faerie is very near to you there.

In case you are wondering how my experience felt, well, I was frankly disbelieving at the time. 'How can this be the Otherworld?' I kept asking my familiar. 'This doesn't seem very different from usual – except more beautiful than most places. I must be having a fantasy. Or you're having a laugh!'

The ground was solid under my feet and I felt the summer breeze on my face. The drystone wall was solid to touch and the seasons certainly had not reversed. I thought, 'How lucky people are around here; to have such a beautiful stretch of unspoilt countryside on the edge of their town. And only five minutes from the High Street. Wow!' I did not know that the farmland through which I was walking no longer existed. Nowadays, the area is covered by many modern houses. I later discovered them to have been built in the 1980s. Almost twenty years before I walked there, the place had already been covered by a new estate. In fact, that was what gave the game away. I had noticed those modern houses before I went through the portal. And I knew that once I had emerged from the yard of the little factory they should again have been visible. But they were not.

No doubt, many people would have been braver than I at this point. Or been less well advised by a familiar. Some may even have felt that they had less to lose. But I had a husband and two adult children, a mother then still living, some very dear friends, and also work – both magical and literary – with which I am passionately involved.

Life in this World can be very painful, even for someone as lucky as I seem to be. There have been times when I have felt that I had had quite enough of it. (I imagine most of us have felt that way, at times.) Nevertheless, when faced with the fact that I might never get back to the life I am currently living, I turned and ran. After just five or ten minutes strolling through the Otherworld, I finally believed my familiar when he said I should hurry up in case the portal closed behind me. I hurtled back the way I had come and into the living World. More than an hour of this World's time had passed during my very brief walk in the realm of elsewhere.

Later, I did my research into the history of the area and came up with my evidence that I had not had a fantasy. For how could I fantasize about buildings I had never heard of, but which had actually existed, even if long ago? This proves nothing except that I may have time-travelled. I am aware of this possibility, of having 'merely' time-travelled. It is not possible that I had read of these historical proofs previously – and then unconsciously remembered them. I had not been living in the area long enough for that, and the buildings were not famous enough to have been known anywhere but in that small town.

It is impossible, in this World, to walk the same way anymore. It has been thus for ages. The way is barred by garden fences and a bowling green and an old pavilion. However, I did it. And I think this shows how much the map of the Otherworld is both within the land and inside ourselves.

The biggest surprise to me was that it felt natural in Faerie. I was entirely at home there. Granted, the landscape looked quite magical as well as very beautiful. But round here, that is not to be wondered at. The land often seems to be drifting almost out of manifestation for there is almost always a light mist, a haze, a diffuseness in the air. It is this characteristic look that can make the island of Britain seem to be a region of Faerie, even in this World.

But – to get back to my glimpse of history – is the Otherworld simply the past?

Not according to tradition. Time runs differently there, so the past has a lot to do with it. But Faerie is not this World at an earlier date. Nor is it an exact mirror image of how this World once was. As I have said, there are differences as well as similarities. You both can and cannot map it according to the geography of our World. For one thing, the terrain of a place can be altered physically by time. Coastal erosion, earth tremors, human activity and climate change can profoundly alter a landscape anywhere in this World. In some places, the Dorset coast used to be two miles further south than it is now. Whole villages have gone below the sea in Norfolk and Suffolk. The past of a place, as physical country, may be completely unrecognizable when compared with the same place now. More importantly, that aspect of the Otherworld I visited is shaped partly by the memories of the dead themselves. (The map of the Otherworld is also within those who live there; it is not only within the visiting person such as myself.) It is shaped by the love of the dead for the places they knew. I was told this by my familiar when I complained about having seen a little country church in the Otherworld.

'What was that doing in Faerie?' I stormed at him later. 'I don't want to see anything to do with big human institutions like the Church or the State!'

'Well, you will have to put up with it,' he replied, mildly. 'The place where you went is made of all that the dead can remember with love and which they found beautiful. And many did love their village church and its graveyard. It was where they married and named their children and buried their dead. And not all parsons were ranting misogynists. Not all wanted to burn their local wisewomen and cunning men at the stake. Many people found comfort at such places and were given strength.'

Yes, of course. They found their local church beautiful, not only as a building, but because of what it stood for – or some did.

My familiar went on to explain:

'There are other parts of the Otherworld that have been shaped by human memories, but without any love. These are not beautiful. And yet others that are a mixture of beauty and ugliness remembered by those whose lives were harsh. Such places shift, separate or mingle qualities and appearances, according to the perceptions and experiences of the dead, as well as according to changes in their inner attitudes while in the Otherworld. There are also places not shaped, even partly, by the dead or by living humans, but mainly by faerie species who never incarnate in your World. Underlying all this is the fact that all places are shaped by the primal spirits of land, sea and sky, the spirits of the elemental forces of rock and water, fire and ice and space and air. It is they who shape any land uninhabited by conscious, sentient beings. In all that we do by way of shape-shifting the land through our actions and memories, we are shaped by them. Human and faerie alike, we are shaped by the land and its primal spirits every bit as much as we do the shaping. That is because we are of the land, wherever we are. We are of Nature. Humans don't like that idea. We know that in Faerie. A great many humans like to think that their kind is in charge of it all – or soon will be. Ha! They've a lot to learn. Well, we shall see what becomes of them – shan't we?'

Oh, yes (Great Mother help us!) we shall see that eventually.

He is very articulate, the elf who has become my familiar. When we first met, he was not so adept in his understanding of human concepts and perspectives, especially those of the present day. But he is now both insightful and fluent, as is my faerie teacher. The Fae learn how to communicate with us in our current languages by observing our thought patterns and simply sensing the meaning while listening to us. In this way, they can learn to speak colloquially and well. However, in the early stages of a faerie–human relationship, they more usually transmit ideas straight into our minds in a way that is beyond words. It is a completely non-verbal form of communication, but our own minds supply the words as we grasp what is being intended.

Actually, the Fae are believed to talk among themselves in a form very different from human language. (The same has been said about the human dead.) The seventeenth-century expert on the matter, Robert Kirk, had this to say on the subject in his book, *The Secret Commonwealth of Elves, Fauns and Fairies.*

'They speak but little and that by way of whistling, clear, not rough.'

Myself, I can often hear the sounds of faerie conversation. The whistling seems to me to be high pitched. The notes are very short and distinct and come in quick succession, hundreds of them, rapid and silvery. When I hear this, I know that the Fae have a great deal to communicate. Not necessarily to me, but I am privileged to hear them for it means that the veil between the Worlds has thinned for some reason. Either that or I am 'between the Worlds' in regard to my state of consciousness, as are the Fae, at times of their own choosing, when they have work to do with us or with our dimension of the Earth.

This is not difficult to grasp when we think of what has been said about the Otherworld and its location. For example, the nineteenth-century researcher W.Y. Evans-Wentz remarked in his book *The Faery Faith in Celtic Countries* that the Celts believed that the Otherworld is 'interpenetrated' with this one. He meant that it is not even a breath or a heartbeat away; it is a change of dimension distant, but one that is right here.

Dr Ramses Saleem, a present-day expert on Egyptian religion, tells us much the same about his country's ancient beliefs. In the Egypt that pre-dated Christianity or Islam, the Otherworld was believed to be interpenetrating this one, even though it was invisible and, for most of the living, inaccessible. So far, so good. The Otherworld's geography is linked with the land itself, and with the whole Earth and the physical cosmos we live in. In shape-shifting terrain, this is all that we can really have as a map of the Otherworld, for certain.

Scientists tell us there is something hard-wired into this World's reality that is called the Heisenberg Uncertainty Principle. This explains how the real behaviour of particles can never be pinned down completely, not at the quantum level of life. They say that the harder you look at them, the fuzzier their ways will seem to become. It is as though Nature is designed to conceal her ultimate secrets. The Otherworld, though not reducible to 'just quantum reality' is exactly like that. So the old forgotten maps of Faerie are both simple and total Mystery. The real maps will always be those that the heart knows and cannot quite put into words.

Lizzie Webfoot knows the Heartland of Faerie and its maps quite well. So does Johnnie Hoof. Heartfelt truths are at the core of the magic these two experience and practise.

Mrs Eldridge knows some humans disdain the heart-truths of Faerie and all its chancy and unmappable gates. They would like to put the laws of Nature under human control everywhere on Earth and banish Mystery. The idea makes her blood run cold, even though she knows that they cannot actually do that – in either World. She also knows that many attempts have been made by living humans to understand the regions or subdivisions of Faerie. (This is in order to navigate rather than to control or subdue them.) But what makes some of these ideas or symbols most valuable is that they can be used to deepen our sense of connection with the Otherworld. The best way to do this is just to let the mind play dreamily with ideas about what realms there might be in the Otherworld according to ancient symbols or glyphs – until conscious-ness deepens and connections are seen.

In Hebrew and Kabalistic cosmology, there are seven Otherwordly realms. The Tibetan Bardo contains three basic divisions, but within these there are many others. The Irish Otherworld seems to have five realms, while to the Nordic and Germanic peoples there were three, each divided into three, making nine realms in all.

The main and most popular perception all over the World is that, however you subdivide them, and whether or not you include them all in your idea of Faerie, there are three realms in the Otherworld:

The realm which corresponds to the Soul of the living World – this is the one in which you may find earthbound spirits, 'house elves' (traditionally called brownies, boggarts, hobgoblins or hobthrusts) and many other beings (including, according to Northern European beliefs, both dwarves and giants). Some have suggested that these are ways of naming the spirits of natural features such as underground rock formations (dwarves) and huge mountain ranges (giants).

The realm which corresponds to the Soul of the Heavens – most indigenous tribespeople throughout the World are thought to have believed that the dead are borne upwards towards the stars, especially such people who have lived honourably and attained wisdom. To the tribes of the past, it may have seemed that constellations of stars actually touched the Earth as they rose over the horizon. These were linked with, or seen as being, particular Goddesses and Gods. Perhaps these Deities were thought to create a portal for spirits to enter so they could reach a divine dimension. In mytho-poetic terms, this does seem likely. People may also have thought that the ancestral realm was literally in the sky. That is to say, they may have thought that it was physically above us in *this* World, a view that was certainly held by some Christians when I was a child, though it is a belief that is pre-Christian in origin.

The realm which corresponds to the Soul of the Underworld – here dwell the dead who await either an ascent to the realm of light or a reincarnation in this World. To Christians, this realm was demonized as an evil place where wrong-doers were tortured. To Northern European Pagans, it was more a place of renewal, where the cauldron of Lady Hel brought forth new life – for her fires were transformative and healing. To the ancient Egyptians, it was the place through which all the dead had to pass for purification, healing and transformation, and the passage was very testing. For a corrupt spirit, it could result in a permanent end to their existence. The raw materials of what had once been them would then be purified and transformed (in a way, composted), becoming at one with Nature within the Otherworld – just as the body of a dead person becomes at one with Nature here, within this World. New life forms would then arise.

The beliefs of some British traditional witches are rather like this, for they say that individual survival of death is not the fate of every person even though nothing is lost and all is renewed in some way or another. In Faerie lore, the plants and creatures in our World share a group soul for they are not individuated. Each one belongs to the soul of their species to such an extent that individual survival cannot exist. The death of a rose bush can be followed by the growth of a new one, but not, of course, as a personal reincarnation of that same plant. There are also said to be some species of the Fae who are not individuated, but who share a group soul. Others, however, have individuality of their own, just as a human being may. Or as, arguably, some members of other species might achieve. Dogs? Horses? Dolphins? Elephants? Cats? Individuation is the most precious thing. But, of course, it carries its own dangers for it is where innocence is lost. (An individual has his or her own agenda and own choices – at least, to some extent. But a member of a group soul cannot make a moral decision and is never therefore personally responsible for anything. On the other hand, an individual person has accountability. The issue is complicated by the fact that as individuals we also each share the group soul of our race and our species.) Traditional witches believe that for some human beings individuation has not developed. These cannot individually survive death.

But to get back to the subject of how the Otherworld is arranged, we can see that all over the World in just about every culture, there is the wonderful symbol called the World Tree. This image shows not only the three realms (however subdivided), but also the links that exist between them. All living creatures are around the trunk of an imagined mighty tree that reaches all the way to the stars. The Heavens are represented by the stars themselves, seen amongst the topmost branches. The Underworld is below the land among the Tree roots.

Alternatively, the World Tree can show the relationship of the two Worlds, with this World being seen everywhere above the land's surface and the Otherworld being underground among the Tree roots or upon them. (In the Norse version, there are nine sub-worlds within the Otherworld. Three mighty roots bear three worlds each.) This image is an important one for it shows the interdependence of this World and the Otherworld. The whole Tree must be healthy for either World to flourish. However, there are many trees – such as the yew, willow and elder – which can regenerate from the roots if the living tree is cut down. And also some trees can grow new roots if so much as a staff or an old branch is stuck in the ground. This seems to teach that either World holds something of the pattern of the other within itself.

Symbol or glyph (or, in the East, a mandala) showing the Otherworld in relation to this World – that is all the map you get! Plus, an idea of what you might expect to find between lives according to Faerie lore or other systems . . . something poetic and enigmatic describing something real, but of absolute Mystery. In that respect, it is exactly like this World we live in, where Mystery also prevails, to the joy of some and the distress of others.

CHAPTER FOUR

FAERIE TYPES AND PURPOSES

My teacher in all things magical is of the Fae. She belongs to a species that does not incarnate in this World (or not anymore), but lives always in the Otherworld as its natural home. Such beings are not immortal. They just have a far longer life span than do humans. When they die, they go to a place where there is a great lake of golden fire that does not burn anyone; to be immersed in it brings renewal and joy. Thus refreshed, the faerie spirit is then re-born into the Otherworld to a faerie mother – or so my faerie teacher says.

Their lifespans are immensely long – many thousands of years of our time for some of their species – yet they are not immortal. I make this point because some who begin on the Faerie path may take faerie guidance as though it were ultimate wisdom and may even take faerie teachers as beings who exist solely to guide and teach human beings. This is a serious mistake as the Fae each have their own plans and purposes other than helping humans. They are by no means Pagan precursors of the Christian guardian angel and many regard the solipsism of the human species with awe (and with some disgust). Also, the Fae are fallible. My faerie teacher has asked me to make this clear.

'We are all fallible who live in this World or the Other,' she says. 'We are all travellers through the Worlds for the sake of our evolution towards greater wisdom and greater harmony.'

She adds that while faerie values can seem a lot saner to fey people than human ones – and while some of faeriekind are far more advanced in knowledge and wisdom – only the Great Mother knows everything. This is because She is the sum total of all spirit in all the Worlds. She is that which gives birth to spirit and She is all spirit. So She does not have universal consciousness – She is universal consciousness. She is the great balancing, harmonizing and evolutionary power that runs through all things. Some call Her Goddess; some, God; some, Fate . . . Destiny, Mystery, Wyrd or Nature's Alchemy. Any individual faerie or human or creature of any kind may convey some of Her wisdom, but no one has it all. 'Therefore,' says my teacher, 'trust your Otherworldly kin and teachers and friends as much, at least, as you would trust their equivalents in your own World. But always retain your right and responsibility to gain your own wisdom. Treasure it and hone it, your own heart's wisdom. It may take countless numbers of lives, or all the time that exists to bring it to fruition, but that is what you exist for. And it is not the job of the Fae to gain that wisdom for you. We can share what we know but that is all.'

That is the kind of thing my faerie teacher tells me. She is not pretentious about the things that she knows, and she can be quite sharp when her patience is tried too far.

I see her clairvoyantly. She has long black hair and pale skin and dark green eyes with silver flecks. She wears a long white dress that is patched and pied with black. Her feet are slightly and almost transparently webbed. They are quite small. In fact, she is small and finely made all over.

But she is not tiny. (About four feet high, I should think.)

Faerie woman of her kind use their magic for many purposes, but one is to help keep the whole web of Nature in balance and harmony. They do this in their own World, but the effect is passed to this World because the Worlds are different dimensions of one Whole. Some do it by dancing. I have often watched them using movement and dance magically to bring good health to the sea, land, sky and all forms of life. I do not know why, but they always seem to be near water when I see them do this work – near the sea or a big lake. I see them in visions, their movements like a slow-motion ballet. Always fluid and graceful, they can flip easily through a slow series of cartwheels and arabesques before pacing up the sheer face of a high cliff. It is as though they need not concern themselves with gravity. They do their healing, balancing and transformative magic by a merging of their own spirits with the cliffs, oceans, land, trees, animal species – whatever they like. They do this psychically and with ease. Then by the harmony and balance of their dance, they enhance the strength and balance of what is all around them while themselves being strengthened and renewed by the land, sea and sky with which they are at one.

My faerie teacher is of a kind similar to the magical dancer, but she does her work by enchantment rather than by dancing, chanting her spells for the good health of the land, particularly for the inland waters and for the trees.

She and I have been together through many of my own lifetimes. Indeed, I would not have liked to live in this World without being able to hear her gentle, though sometimes formidable, advice.

What type of the Fae are these magical dancers? Or my own faerie teacher in her harlequin dress? She says that she can be called a vala or fay because her business is the weaving of Fate – with words. A type of faery witch, then. She is concerned with spells – so are the dancers in their own way.

She says that she lives in something called 'The Lake Realm in the Hill'. This means she comes from a place where the dead are healed and renewed. But not just the humans. Here, the dead plants and creatures are also tended before being returned to the group soul of their own species in preparation for a new life. The place is not macabre; it is beautiful. (I have seen it for myself in visions.)

Many attempts have been made in our World to describe the Fae as a type on the basis of moral or value judgements, but too often human fears or desires can confuse the issue. For there is no doubt that we in this World have projected many of our own traits or fantasies upon faerie beings. Thus, they have been seen as being wildly, insatiably erotic, voracious, thieving and vengeful by some of humankind. There is equally no doubt that some in the Otherworld do have these tendencies, but generalizations are as likely to mislead us in Faerie as they do in our own World, where there are words for that kind of thing. (Racism, for example.)

By the time we have pushed aside the human desire for kindly faerie godmothers to nurture, cosset and spoil us, as well as having pushed aside our fear of the unknown and perhaps desire for a scapegoat, we are left with the fact there are many types and species in Faerie, from *leprechauns* to *light-elves*, from the *peri* to the *pwcca* and so on, all around the World. And that many of them have very strong personalities and can always surprise. However, classifications can be of value and bring an increase in understanding if we are not too rigid about how we apply them. The only real alternative is the 'long list' approach, showing faerie types from around the

World alphabetically. For this, I recommend Anna Franklin's excellent book *The Illustrated Encyclopedia of Fairies*. There are also books by the late K.M. Briggs that are legendary, but these can be difficult to get hold of at present.

When it comes to broad categories, I like the scheme set out by Orion Foxwood in *The Faery Teachings*, as it is based in ancient lore. Here, we have the following.

Solitary faeries are beings such as the house spirit – traditionally, in Britain, called a brownie, hobgoblin or hobthrust.

Or they are faeries attached to particular families, such as the bean sidhe, who warns of an imminent death.

Or they are faeries attached to particular places, such as the white lady, guardian of a healing well or spring. Or the kelpie, a faerie horse who lives in the sea and is dangerous if you mount him as he tends to carry people out of their depth with a view to drowning them!

Hive faeries are faery groups who make up one being between them in the same way that bees make up one swarm. It is said that they can easily cross into our World, and often do. Their presence is announced by a cold wind that seems to come up from the ground, or by the sound of buzzing, rather like bees. They tend to be ruled by a queen and she consists of all her subjects merged together as one. In spite of the chill wind which heralds them, hive faeries are believed to bear goodwill towards humankind (usually).

In Scotland, there are two types of *trooping faery*: those who bring blessings, and those who cause harm. The beneficent troops are called 'the seelie court' and the baneful ones, 'the unseelie court'. The word 'seelie' comes from the Anglo-Saxon *selig*, meaning 'holy'.

In England, trooping faeries are not so much seen as

'good' versus 'bad', but as those who bring the blessings of fertility and good health compared with those who banish what is unhealthy (or even take away the souls of the dead to the Otherworld). These last are sometimes called The Wild Hunt. They ride out into our World at the old Celtic festival of Samhain (31 October) while the green-clad summer troop rides out at Beltaine (30 April/1 May).

The Norse Valkyries – faerie women who also carry the dead to the Otherworld – are another troop, though they can act individually as well.

The *stationary Fae* are linked with one place, and are called 'stationary' because they do not ever travel far away from it. However, the term does not mean that these faeries stand still. Like the magical dancers (who are not, however, stationary), they look after or perhaps guard a particular site such as a forest, a hill, a pool, a cave, or even a single tree. They are of the type often called 'Nature spirits', a term I reject as it seems to imply that everything else is either not of Nature or does not possess a spirit. Whereas, in the animistic beliefs that underlie our Faerie tradition, everything has a spirit and everything is of Nature, even man-made things, since humankind is a product of Nature and so are the raw materials worked with by humans.

In every land on Earth, these 'Nature spirits' or guardians have been known to each human tribe or culture. Undoubtedly, some of the folklore concerning them is about an anthropomorphic image of the spirit (energy pattern) of the actual pool, cave, river, forest or whatever. In that sense, they are not actually of the Fae at all, but are of the living places and entities within our own World. Other lore may depict an Otherworldly resident of a particular place or indicate a spot favoured by visitors from Faerie. These, though linked with a place through circumstances or choice are unlikely to be stationary in the sense of unable to move more than, say, a few hundred yards. (In the same way, a caretaker of a building in our World may not go very far in the course of his work, but he can move). However, the writer R.J. Stewart tells us in his book *The Living World of Faery* that emigrants from Britain and Ireland to America or Australia have often found that their faerie allies were not prepared to go with them, overseas. Some would and some would not. Therefore, some of the Celtic healers and seers of the nineteenth century (and of more recent times) had to make new friendships with those from amongst the faerie population of their new country.

So, when is a stationary fae not really stationary?

Categorization is never easy. Many of the Fae transcend any real pigeon-holing at all. This is partly because they can shift shape or appear in disguise. It is also because they may belong to more than one type. In this, they are not unlike humans. For instance, I am British and fey. I am also a vegetarian and a writer. But there are many British people who are not fey and many people of other nations who most definitely are. Also, there are vegetarians in many parts of the World and they are not necessarily fey. Most writers are probably meat eaters and neither fey nor British. And so on. So I belong to at least four categories – well, probably dozens, actually!

Categorization is worthwhile. It can teach us a lot. But if we view any one of the Fae as just a type, one particular type, and then say, 'That's all there is to know', we will be wrong and unpopular. (No one likes to be stereotyped in either of the Worlds.)

When it comes to meetings that people have had with faeries while in this World, encounters with eyes wide open and seeing what was right there before them rather than in visions, there seem to be just two categories. First, there are those faeries who appear earthy and very solid. Some of them are quite small and look rather like those depicted in the art of Brian Froud, the painter of Faerie. They often have clothes in earthy shades of brown or green or russet. And brown, leathery skin and the pointed ears that are traditional. Sometimes, their clothes are ragged and their hair full of leaves and feathers. Others, like the West Country pixies, are dressed in bright colours. Red and blue or bright green, perhaps. But always, they are solid, creaturely, as we are.

The other type consists of beings of light. They seem to be made out of nothing but coloured light, all the shades of the rainbow. For example, in Kilver Court Garden, Shepton Mallet, I have seen a tall faerie woman of light that was green – or green blended with gold. She was standing in the small lake. It is not very deep. Perhaps she was the lake guardian? Those who guard wells or springs or pools are green or white, it is said. The Lady of this particular lake was happy to talk for a while. She counselled me to bless the waters of the river Sheppey, which feed her lake: bless them with good health, good fortune and purity. She also suggested that I bless all the underground lakes and streams in the area. One of these lakes provides drinking water for all the East Mendip towns and villages. In her view, people can sometimes help to heal and protect lakes and rivers in very simple ways. (Of course, it helps if a lot of people do this kind of thing and do it often.) It supplements the work that she and her kind do from their own dimension.

Faeries who seem to be made of light and nothing more are commonly seen. The mystic George William Russell (whose pen name was 'A.E.') described those he saw as being of two kinds. He called them the Shining Beings and the Opalescent Beings. The Shining Beings were of the 'hive' type, while the Opalescent ones were individuals and of a very high spiritual development – far higher and more harmonious than that of human beings. He saw them in nineteenth-century Ireland and believed them to be of the race called the Sidhe. He said that their home in the Otherworld was called *Tir-na-nog* and that it is a radiant archetype of this World containing only harmony and beauty. In this, it sounds quite similar to the English version of the Otherworld known as Avalon: a place where there is no sorrow or sickness and in which the blossom, fruit and leaves adorn all the trees all the year round.

George William Russell believed that anyone who saw the *Sidhe* during his life and who thought about them a lot would be likely to go to their World after death. He also believed that more than one Otherworld existed, though he may have meant that there was more than one realm in just the one Otherworld. In any event, he said that there were places where only ugliness prevailed and he seems to have believed they were the result of egotism. In contrast, among the higher orders of the Irish Fae, it was usual to have a sense of connectedness with others and to be linked in unity with the forces of Nature, ego having been transcended. He said there seemed to be no sense of constraint about it. They were joyful. Egotism he saw as always destructive of beauty within the Otherworld – and presumably destructive of joy, as well.

I asked my faerie teacher whether the Beings of light that I have seen are called Shining ones or Opalescent ones but she did not understand my question. 'To us, they are just called Ladies of Well and Wood,' she replied. 'And the men are called Lords of the Paths between the Worlds. Their work is to bring forth golden light from our World into yours for good health and renewal.'

'But what type are they?'

'They are from the Lake realm in Faerie.'

On further questioning, this seemed to mean the place now known to many English people as Avalon.

This seems to confirm my feeling that those Fae seen by George William Russell are indeed the same type or types, but by another name. However, I must add that those whom I have seen in vision as solid and clad in black and white or in green or red are also living in the Lake realm – or so I am told. So once again, generalizations are a mistake. Obviously, there are many types living in that realm. And it is also said that those who appear to us made out of light in this World may be quite solid within their own.

There are many traditional ways of contacting the Fae. My advice is very simple. Go to a beautiful place where you know you can be alone – that is, free from interruption. You can go with a friend so long as that person is comfortable with what you are doing and, preferably, is a believer in Faerie; otherwise, they could spoil the experience for you without intending to.

You might choose a forest, a deserted beach, a hilltop or a lakeside – anywhere that you sense has a good psychic atmosphere, and which you find uplifting.

Bless the Fae of that place with good health, peace and well-being. Bless them in the names of Mother Earth and the Green God of Nature, or in the name of the Great Mother.

Ask them to befriend you and to bless you with some contact with them.

Sit or stand quietly and see if you can sense any response. Do you see a sudden flickering of light or hear a whispered word or an inner message? However fleeting or ephemeral it may seem to be, do not dismiss it, for it is a kind of beginning. If you feel nothing, you can always try again another time or at another place. This is not something you can only do once. It is informal and can be done whenever you feel you would like to try it.

When you feel ready, thank the Fae (whether you were aware of them or not) and leave the place.

Oddly enough, some traditional lore states that you should never thank the Fae for anything that they do for you as it gives offence. Myself, I have never found that courtesy seems offensive to anyone from either World and I feel more comfortable thanking them than not. Dear reader, you must decide for yourself about this. But please remember that some traditional prohibitions (such as that against eating or drinking anything which has been ritually offered to the Fae or the dead) may be important. In fact, the breaking of that particular rule is said to bring very bad luck.

Traditional ways of meeting the Fae are said to include the following.

1. Sitting in an elder grove at midnight during the Summer Solstice.
2. Picking a wild rose that grows near to a well or spring.
3. Going to an old burial mound, particularly at dawn or at dusk.

Wherever you go to make a contact, there is no substitute for reaching out to the Fae by talking to them, either out loud or inside yourself. But remember, we need to give them something. They do not like those whose aim is to just take and take, so tradition tells us. Instead, they are said to look favourably on simple gifts like a blessing or a song. In fact, singing for the Fae is a very good way to make initial contact. Even if you feel that your singing voice is not especially good, they will still appreciate that you made the effort.

Go to a quiet place outside such as a wood or a hilltop

and tell them, 'I offer this'. Then sing your song and afterwards ask for their friendship and blessing. You can make up your own words and sing them to your own tune. Alternatively, you can sing an old folksong, particularly one from the area or land where you are. My song might go something like this. (You are welcome to use it if you like. . . .)

Hale to the Fae of this place,
kindly and good. Hale to you all.
By water and wood, I ask in the name
of the Great Faerie Queen
to be seen as I am,
a friend from my heart.
I ask for your friendship.
By magical art, may I be protected
from each kind of harm.
befriended by you
who are kindly and calm,
kept safe from each bane
by a faerie charm.

Now place on the ground a bowl of fresh water and a small piece of wood. Later, when you leave, pour out the water, but keep the wood. Traditionally, apple, hawthorn and rowan are the best for invoking faerie contact. Or you can use that famous combination of oak, ash and hawthorn. (A master or mistress of faery magic might bring a wand made of one of these woods, but actually just twigs will do if the making of a wand feels beyond you for now.) If the woods of first choice are not available, you can fall back on elder, hazel, birch or wild rose. And if, reader, you feel too shy to sing out loud, even when alone, you can just speak the words, after all.

Some of our ancestors seem to have been more concerned about avoiding contact with Faerie. Folklore abounds with prescriptions against being abducted or pestered by them.

1. Keep something made of iron under your pillow at night.
2. Ring bells at the faerie.
3. Refrain from singing in any place where the Faes might dwell.
4. Block your ears if you hear faerie music or you might pine away and die.
5. Carry some ground-ivy or (on May Eve) wear a daisy chain.
6. Turn your clothes inside out – especially if you are being led out of your way by pixies while out on a walk.
7. Make an equal-armed cross of rowan wood tied with red thread and keep it next to your bed. (Perhaps this invokes the wrath of good faeries against bad ones. And since such crosses are sacred – traditionally, to Brigid, a Pagan Goddess who is also a Faerie Queen – it would seem so.)

Myself, I have found that some of those here in the living World of humankind present much more of a threat than do the Fae. (Well, what with wars, environmental destruction, robbery, rape, fraud, etc., what else can we conclude?) In any case, if you are kind and courteous towards those of the Otherworld, you are likely to meet with kindliness in return. Many a folk and faery tale such as 'Mother Holle' and 'The Well at the World's End' make this point clear.

Before we leave the subject of how to meet faeries, I must add that many people have seen them spontaneously. They have neither sought for such an experience nor guarded against it. I expect that most of them, perhaps all, were country dwellers and were out in the fields or woods in the course of their work, or for some other reason.

Some recent encounters of this kind are described by Jon Dathen in his book *Somerset Faeries and Pixies*. It is the work of a present-day folklorist who has done his field-work as well as any of his nineteenth-century predecessors, and discovered that under the surface of our modern World, the British are just as aware of the Fae and of the magic that lurks in our countryside as our ancestors were, whether fearfully or not.

I asked my faerie teacher why so many people have thought Otherworldly experiences are dangerous. There are many tales about people who have languished and died as a result of a visit to the Otherworld or even after listening to faerie music or hearing faerie voices while still in this World. I told my teacher:

'They say that the living can pine away with longing for Faerie if they have once seen it or heard its music.'

'Well, you have not done so,' she reminds me. 'But there will always be some people who find the living World too harsh or who have too few ties of love to make them want to stay there. Such souls can be very vulnerable to the call of our World. And even if they had no contact with Faerie at all, they might still be inclined to long for something other than their own life. There is a great deal of suffering in your World. And yet you must realize that there have not been so many people who died from contact with the Otherworld as those who died for lack of it. Many cases of suicide could have been prevented by an awareness of us. So many suffer a psychic barrenness, numbness and isolation of spirit. Sometimes, it is quite dreadful to behold: for some of these, a bright vision of the beauty of Faerie and the sound of our music could have brought healing to their wounded hearts. And then they might have flourished and lived on. And yet living humans have thought of Faerie as though it were alluring but toxic, some kind of glamorous but fatal drug.'

'For some of them, perhaps it has been.'

'Our World can be what you make of it.'

'Just like the living World where sometimes that's very true?'

'Yes, it is true. Indeed.'

Contact with Faerie has certainly helped me and many of my friends to live more joyfully. Visions of beauty, wise guidance and an exchange of blessings have enhanced my life. And I think it can help us to recognize this World's beauty if we have had contact with Faerie, however fleeting. Somehow, it can open our eyes. But as my faerie teacher has said, a contact with the Otherworld (or the lack of that) is something to which people respond according to their own character. Human types and purposes are as important as faerie ones in determining the outcome.

To me, one of their greatest gifts has been the imparting of their philosophy – as in the following dialogue.

RAE   You have told me that we may not ask the Fae to be wise for us, as though we were their children, but should each strive to gain our own wisdom. How may we best do that?

FAERIE   All that you ask for sincerely is always given by the Great Mother, She who is Queen of Fate and the Soul of Nature. Sooner or later, you will become more wise or more loving or more psychic – or whatever you really want – if you ask for that from your heart. You may or may not like the process by which it comes to you so it is always best to ask that you may make your gain without harming anyone, even yourself. But insincere asking does not work. It is your *desire* for wisdom that brings it to you.

RAE   But my desire is that you should guide me – as

	for so many years, for so many lives you have always done. Or if not that, I desire that you should always be my friend and let me, well, compare notes with you. Anyway, I feel there is more to it than what you have just told me.
FAERIE	Of course there is! To gain wisdom in the Great Mother's name, you need to know that it is first found in the place where you are standing, within the land, in the Soul of Nature.
RAE	Even in a city?
FAERIE	Yes, even there.
RAE	What should I do with that knowledge?
FAERIE	Ask the Faerie Queen of that area to help you with your quest. But first, if you are in your house, light a candle in offering to her. Bless her realm and all who live in it with love and truth and beauty. (For these are the three aspects of wisdom.) Bless in the names of the Great Mother and of the Lord who is Her lover and other Self. Tell her that you are seeking wisdom and ask her to bless you with what you seek without any harm to yourself or to others.
RAE	Why? I mean, wouldn't her knowledge be limited, her wisdom untried beyond her own area?
FAERIE	Yes. But she is linked with each Faerie Queen and King throughout your whole land in just the same way that your own area is a part of your entire island – the land of Britain. And these are all Otherworldly resonances of much greater powers – Mother Earth and the Green God of Nature (as are all Faery Queens and Kings in all the lands upon Earth). And these, Mother Earth and the Green God, are held within the greater

61

pattern of Sun, Moon and stars along with all planets within the solar system and so also connected with all in this galaxy and in this universe. Therefore, through your local Faerie queen, you are linked with the Soul of Nature Everywhere. But in any case, you are not asking her to give you her wisdom, only to help you in the quest for your own.

RAE　　But why be so complicated? Why not just ask the Great Mother, as you suggested at first? Why bless the area in which I live or ask the local Faerie Queen to help me with this?

FAERIE　Because it brings a different result. Without it, you would not feel your connection with the Great Soul of Nature because you would have failed to link with it all around you and under your feet, the soul of your very own locality, a part of the soul of your land and this planet Earth. Therefore, you would have made of the Great Mother an abstract thing. You would have tried to reach beyond your local Fae and the ancestral spirits and all the faery plants and creatures and also ignored the sacredness of your own living reality – its meaning, its own Mystery. For the two Worlds are one and so are all beings in each of the Worlds. One interdependent reality. But you can only reach that knowledge by a heartfelt connection with what is closest to you. All else is theory. Your heart must connect. It cannot do so with an abstraction. Nor can you ever find wisdom without experiencing the interconnectedness of all.

CHAPTER FIVE

MRS ELDRIDGE GOES TO WORK

Mrs Eldridge watches with increasing dismay while humans all around her, on the streets and in cafés, begin to zone out with exhaustion and stress. She knows that quite a lot of them now work a twelve-hour day – without any scheduled meal-breaks. Surely, this is illegal? Or used to be? But even if it still is, that does not seem to make any difference. And, even worse, to live in the human community is to be bombarded with regulations. (At least in Britain, it is, these days.) Rules and propaganda . . . *and* lies.

'Don't put your wheelie bin out for rubbish collection before 7.00 p.m. on the previous night or you may be fined!'

'Return your Income Tax form online by 31 January, or pay a fine!'

'Produce identification – original documents only – if you wish to buy a home. Or else you do not legally exist and must desist!'

'You may not remove your child from school for a

family holiday during term-time without incurring a penalty!'

'Be terrified of terrorists!'

'Be very angry with immigrants!'

'Don't go out busking without a licence!'

'Do not concern yourself about the environment. Looking after it is a luxury, not a necessity. Here, in the real world, we don't bother with that.'

'You need a television or some kind of screen in every room, including the downstairs toilet, the hallway and the potting shed. Failure to comply will be disbelieved!'

'Don't think your own thoughts or relish peace or seek seclusion. Do not enjoy silence nor listen to birdsong. These things are uneconomic and you will be branded an eccentric. Besides, you really ought to be at work or shopping.'

'You should be banking online or by telephone. You should be comparing the prices charged by different energy companies. You should be racking up loyalty points in the supermarket. You should be toeing the line.'

'Don't worry about fracking. Accept all our plans for fracking. It's entirely safe. What? No, of course it won't do the environment any harm. What a funny thing to worry about! Really, you've no cause for concern. *We* always know best. What? Climate change? But we're attending to that. You go back to sleep or go out shopping.'

Beneath this onslaught, some humans have withdrawn their souls within thick shells, rather like offended snails. Mrs Eldridge sees that the shells are composed of numbness and denial. And that they serve to lessen pain and anxiety for the suffering human. But they also, as a result, stop people from asking questions such as: 'What can we do to end this madness?'

Well, what can we do? And whom does all this really

serve? Mrs Eldridge knows the answer, as do most people. But she thinks we will not see this World become a saner place without help from the Otherworld. So standing in the moonlight on a small hill, she calls out to the healing powers of the Fae.

Suddenly, there is a voice in the hiss and whistle of elvish conversation. One of the Fae is speaking in English. She stands beside Mrs Eldridge in the moonlight looking like a woman made of white mist. But her voice is clear and strong and she says this.

'Ask that your heart be at one with the healing heart of Faerie, where there is a healing spell for every ill and the light shines golden up from the land – as though it were lit from within by the Earth Herself. Then ask that the power of the Faerie Queen shall arise within you to bring new harmony by strong enchantment.'

Mrs Eldridge does as she is bid, and then she raises her hawthorn wand. Lizzie Webfoot watches all this from the half-darkness of the hedgerow where she stands, learning the ropes. She sees what is going on in this World and in the Other; sees Mrs Eldridge and also sees – with the eyes of her soul – the same faerie visions that are shown to the other woman.

Now Mrs Eldridge holds a crow feather in her other hand. (She has produced it with a flourish from the band of her hat, where it usually lives.) Waving it in the still night air, she calls out to her friends, the crows. This is night-time. They are all gone to roost so surely she will not be successful? But suddenly crows seem to be everywhere: dark-winged beings like shadows flying across the paleness of the moon.

They are crows from Faerie and they fly down to the land, towards something that looks like very long, black strands. For lying over the land is a deeper darkness than that of a night sky. It is a kind of black web or net made out of psychic matter; a dark web of fate created by the thoughts and intentions of certain ruthless living people. This web links people and places to itself, binding them to serve its own greedy ends – or, at the very least, not oppose them. Whom does this web serve? Not the land itself or the people – Lizzie can see that. For as the crows lift the web into the air, each tree and late dog-walker and dark field seems to shimmer into a lighter state, as though free again and much more content.

Then there is the distressing smell of rot as the web is moved. It is releasing the smell of its own nature.

Who has woven it?

What is it for?

Who might want to try to bind every field, stream or river or reservoir or creature or plant or person into going along with their agenda, no matter how much harm this might cause to whomsoever?

'Um, let's see,' mutters Lizzie. 'Who, nowadays, is planning to exploit land and water? Who wants what's out here in rural England?

'Underground, perhaps, the thing they are seeking? A kind of mineral resource? Solid or liquid or . . . could it be . . . gas? Hmmn!'

But she knows the identity of these people and all the details of their plans matter very little, in practice. 'When cleaning the floor, we don't stop to ask how the muck got there,' as Mrs Eldridge has taught her. 'Sometimes, something just needs clearing up, and that is that.'

Lizzie watches with interest as the crows fly off with the net, straight into an open portal that is in the side of a nearby hill. Down into Faerie they take the black net and finally drop the whole thing into a deep pit. Down into the crow-black belly of Faerie Earth. And then each bird shifts

its own shape. Swooping down to the land, they transform, and are now seen to be a sombre species of Fae.
Well, they look sombre but there is an almost festive
atmosphere about them as they dance purposefully and in
triumph, widdershins around the dark hole. Each one is
dressed in a sort of blue-black haze, trimmed with black
feathers. They have the gothic beauty of leafless trees,
silhouetted on an evening sky. Shining through their darkness is the white glimmer of stars. They are white flame
seen through black glass. They are black lace beneath silver
moonlight.

These faeries have the most necessary magic. They
change what is ill into what is well. Are they dangerous,
these dark elves? Their cries are sometimes raucous and
harsh. But they chant and bespell with a will. Their songs
begin with themselves, crow and raven, but then include
their allies such as mackerel and gull – all the powers that
deal with corruption. These are the carrion spirits. Their
wands are of alder, a wood with strongly transformative
power when used in magic. Mrs Eldridge joins in with the
song from where she stands in our own World.

The moon rises over the Faerie hills. The Crow-Fae
continue their dance until the magic is done. Warmth
glows up from the pit now, the composting heat of the
Earth's alchemy. Then the red-gold light burns lower until
the heat is that of a blue flame and the crow men and
women lean down to reclaim what is floating up from the
deep pit. It is a pale, silvery-white net.

'What shall they do with this?' wonders Lizzie.

And soon she knows. The Fae become crows again and
lift up the new net to spread across Faerie. At first, it looks
like thin lines of ghost-light lying across the land, all linked
up. Then it begins to shimmer and give off a sweet smell
reminiscent of fresh grass and meadow flowers.

Soon the dawn comes, and beneath the pale morning sun the net changes once again. Now it is no longer ghost-white but rainbow light, radiant and ethereal. Wherever it touches the land there is beauty and life, which spreads gradually. Songbirds thrive; rivers run clear and clean; leaves are verdant green; wild creatures are abundant. Then the rainbow net dissolves in the land for it binds no one. Everywhere it has touched there is harmony, freedom.

And now the rivers and streams, the fields and farms and the human towns of the living World will benefit. For what happens in that part of Faerie is reflected back here. Reflected back into life as, in this case, unharmed farm-land, undamaged woods, creative businesses, healthy wildlife, solar farms, tide turbines – a green economy, a contented people.

Mrs Eldridge lowers her wand.

She has invoked the carrion spirits successfully. If she had not, they would have come anyway, but later – very much later, and long after the dark net had done its work and brought dreadful harm. By the laws of Nature and magic, they are not permitted to come any earlier unless we call to them. But they always do come in the end, the carrion spirits, after an area of land or a species has suffered destruction, whether because of human commercial interests or some other reason. Better to call them in sooner then, thinks Mrs Eldridge; better to call them in to prevent harm.

It is not pleasant to think of the carrion creatures in our own World that feed on rotting meat; nor to think about the bacteria and worms within the land that transform dead leaves and manure into compost. But they do a great service for everyone, ridding the land and the waters of rotting substances and those pestilential creatures that could otherwise cause disease, turning around what is baneful by feeding upon it, transforming it into their own healthy flesh or into fertile soil. The Carrion-Fae can do much the same with corrupt psychic material, the corrupt spirit patterns that would have materialized as harmful events. Mrs Eldridge is wise in her choice of familiars, as Lizzie knows, and fortunate that the Crow-Fae have chosen her, in return. No one summons or controls these beings. In the end, they answer to no one but the Faerie Queen. Mrs Eldridge is honoured to know that the Queen will allow her to wield some Faerie power and that the Crow-Fae trust her and are her allies. They have seen into her heart and know that it is at one with the healing heart of Faerie (at least, in intention). If it were not, she would have put herself in certain danger by calling out to them. Mrs Eldridge knows that. She knows the risks that she runs in this kind of work.

The black shadowy wings circle around and then fly on. By dawn in this World, their work in Faerie has been done.

Lizzie Webfoot thinks about the magic she has just seen. Would it be difficult to perform? And what if you misused it by accident? Such a thin line, sometimes, between healing and destructive meddling! Oh, not in tonight's work, Lizzie is sure of that. But what about on other occasions? Still, it is a magic that is not afraid of the grim side of life.

Well, would it really work? You would have to be doing it with all your heart and soul and really mean it, but that is true of any magic if you want it to be effective.

You would have to have courage and positivity without practising denial about the harsh truths of the situation that you were working to influence or change. However, you would have strong allies from amongst the healing elves – even if they were a bit challenging. You could call to them to help you, like Mrs Eldridge did.

She hears the voice of Mrs Eldridge's faerie teacher again.

'Ask that your heart be at one with the healing heart of Faerie'.

First, last and forever at one with the healing heart of Faerie. That place within the Land of the Dead where change is made that serves the renewal of health and life. If you really had invoked that place and the powers that dwell in it, then your spell would not be endorsed nor would these Fae assist you with it unless the results are likely to be good and healing. There are other kinds of Fae, however, with other intentions. (Not all who dwell in the Otherworld are benign; Lizzie remembers that Mrs Eldridge has taught her this.) So it matters a great deal to whom you call and with what sincerity. It matters a great deal what is in your own heart.

Lizzie Webfoot and Johnnie Hoof are used to questioning the wisdom of what they are doing. They know that power and danger walk hand in hand.

Johnnie Hoof has his own mentor. He knows someone called the Backstreet Wizard. This character, and others like him, each forerunner, has lived in the lanes, byways and backstreets of Britain since time out of mind (and no doubt in other lands, as well). He asserts his influence from behind the main drag of the World's preoccupations. He does not usually bother with an influential position in life. Pursuit of a high mainstream status is something he sees as a distraction from his real business – unless it comes easily and does not get in the way. Dear reader, you may have met him now and then. He could be a garage mechanic or a gardener or a plumber. He could be a museum curator or run a bookshop. He could be an odd-job man or a street entertainer. As for his home, he could live on a canal boat or in a council flat or in – of course – a backstreet terraced house or cottage. Whatever he does, wherever he lives, the Backstreet Wizard does not much like publicity. His reputation for being a dab-hand at magic tends to be a local one, at least in his own lifetime. In so far as he is known further afield, his name is only familiar to other people of the fey kind. He prefers to live a quiet life. Well, he sees enough glamour and excitement in the Otherworld.

Johnnie Hoof is not sure about that. He had thought about running workshops on magical healing – or magical abilities of a good many kinds. Surely there is a place for things like that? A need for them, perhaps? But the Backstreet Wizard just looks down his nose at this. He just carries on with whatever he is doing, such as mending the shed roof, when Johnnie mentions it. Well, he would.

Now he stops for a cup of coffee, and gives Johnnie a few tips about herbal charms for psychic protection. 'See that old fellow there?' he interrupts himself suddenly, gesturing with his cigarette towards the shed corner. 'What do you make of him?'

'Seems all right,' says Johnnie after one surmising look. 'Been here long?'

'Nope. Turned up yesterday. Just an old goblin. Down on his luck, I reckon.'

The goblin (well, hobgoblin actually) goes on peeling strips of bark from a small stick. He is making a new wand from hazel wood to take fishing. He will use it as rod and magical implement in one. He seems to be wearing some kind of old sack for a jacket and a pair of grubby trousers held up with string. He is about the size of a small child, but his skin is dark and leathery and he has shrewd eyes like a wise old man.

'Pour him a dish of milk,' says the Backstreet Wizard. 'Might stay here and help us fix this old roof.'

But both Johnnie and the hobgoblin wander off to the

river bank. Johnnie ties three knots in willow strands when he gets there. These are charms to tie his own life and fate into the service of enchantment. Nothing could be easier to do than this kind of spell. Nor, since he means it whole-heartedly, more life-changing. He would give as much as the Backstreet Wizard has himself given for Otherworldly allies in his magical work. And they are already gathering around him.

He glances at the old hobgoblin, fishing nearby.

'Going back to help him out?'

'Can't. I'm off to where I come from, me old 'ouse. Didn't do no good when I moved on, see?'

'Well. Good luck!'

'Arrh – thank'ee! Good luck to thee, an' all!'

They regard each other for a moment after this exchange. Then Johnnie turns and goes to find Lizzie.

CHAPTER SIX

Excerpts from a Fey Life

What follows is material from my own journals. They are an account of fey experience – but are not a definitive one – there is no such thing.

Tuesday 18 March 2003
There are so many different faerie types all around us and most of the time we don't notice. Even fey people don't always see them because of being preoccupied with things that need to be made or done. (How little time most of us seem to have for tranquil and solitary gazing, or for just sensing what or who might be close by.)

Many of those I see outdoors are in more or less human form but they're made out of light in all colours. These can be very tall – perhaps twelve or fourteen feet high. They wear long cloaks (or that's what their clothes look like). When they go past, the cloaks seem to billow around them. They move very fast.

Others are homelier characters. Once, on a clifftop, I walked past a pixie. He was dressed in red trousers and a blue jacket and wearing a pointed hood. He wasn't interested in me – just going about his own business.

How did I get to be so privileged?

It happens when I am in a place that is both beautiful and natural such as a wood or the top of a cliff. Then, being awed by the beauty, I become quiet inside myself. Then I can easily hear those among the Fae who are my particular friends, and I can often see others around me and sometimes talk with them, too.

Friday 18 April 2003

I have been having a run of bad luck and asked my faerie teacher why this is happening. Her answer was very blunt and direct.

'It is because you have broken your word to us,' she said. 'You promised to be a faery medium, bringing our messages and enchantments into the living everyday World in which you dwell in your body. But so far, all that you have done is to use your contact with us in your practice as a psychic medium to gain guidance for people in living their lives. This is not what you promised to do, as you know.

'What you promised was to be a medium for what we wish to say. This may or may not be what people think that they wish to hear. It will not, for example, be about their own personal love lives or their careers. Much of it is concerned with the human impact on other species and with all the effects your World has on Faerie and that Faerie has on your World.

'We are not punishing you now. No one is punishing you with a run of bad luck. It is just that by breaking your word you have damaged your soul. Faerie is a World where vows are as real as written contracts. Breaking them means breaking your soul in some way or else twisting it – and that twists your fate.

'If your soul is not straightforward in your dealings with us, then your progress in life is not straightforward either. This is not the only thing that rules your fate – which is co-created by all who have brought your circumstances into being – but it is extremely important. If you are false inside, then things go awry. Your fate begins to mirror back your own soul's state. For such as yourself who communicate with us, this happens quickly. Those who live without much depth in the cut and thrust of human affairs can often go many years with a twisted soul and they still prosper. A fey person can't do that. You have conferred with us, with our World, so effects are swifter. I tell you again it is not a punishment. The cause is your own damaged soul. No one hands out bad luck to you. It is just the inevitable result.

'You cannot just take what you want from Faerie, use your connections with us, and then disregard our ancient laws.'

'What shall I do about it?' I ask.

The answer comes: 'Learn more of our World and our reality and speak about it to others. Do this gradually but begin at once.'

Monday 11 August 2003
My faerie teacher said today, 'A fey human should respect him or herself. Those in your own World may sometimes mock what you do and what you believe, but your work of maintaining the psychic connection between the Worlds is life-sustaining. Your visions of us and your knowledge of our teachings pours into humanity's collective soul, bringing a new awareness of the deep meaning and purpose of all the realm of Nature, its sacredness. We want you to speak of us as you have promised to do. But even if you had not, you would still have been doing

something important.

'The work of a fey person – any sensitive, unworldly human – is to make a link of loving awareness between your World and ours. Such people often do this work unwittingly by their soul's orientation towards natural spirituality and by the psychic resonance they create when communing with Nature.

'Between them, these fey people help to heal the psychic damage caused by more shallow preoccupations or by gross, ruthless human thoughts and activities.

'We of the Faerie World would like humans to be more practical than they are about Nature. Exploitation and abuse are not practical at all. In the end, they lead to the breakdown of what all life forms depend upon – the biosphere itself. We want human beings to enjoy sensuality and good times, and also to honour the needs of other species and of the land.

'For this to become the case, human beings need to think more deeply and see the implications of their actions – be more visionary and more aware. It might seem strange to say that the fey humans can help with this, but they are more aware of the deeper aspects of life because they acknowledge death as their ever-present companion. And they speak our language, the language of elves, and that makes all the difference.'

Tuesday 13 September 2005
My faerie teacher told me today, 'When the right time comes around, then the heart's dream can come true. But,' she went on, 'there are those who don't know their own heart's desire so they may be acting against it. This is rather like a woman who doesn't take care of herself or her own unborn child while pregnant. Then the dream can become damaged or, worse, stillborn. The answer is

to try to act in the best interests of your dream; to cease living at odds with your own heart's desire. You may think there are practical reasons why this just can't be done. A lack of money, perhaps, or a lack of time. But these barriers can often be overcome – especially if you ask us to bless you with a solution to your problem, one that harms no one and is harmonious.'

'How do people get to know their own heart's desire?' I asked. 'What's your advice to people who just do not know?'

'Know yourself. Know what brings you joy or brings you a deep, quiet satisfaction. Know what you long for, above all.'

'But supposing your dreams are vicious? You might, for example, long for revenge after being hurt. Or your dream might be just plain greedy, or might depend on abusing or exploiting someone or something.'

'Such bad dreams as these, such nightmares, will only be banished from every heart when all have learned just how unsatisfying it really is when they come true. Increasingly unsatisfying, for they are of the nature of addiction. The feeding of an addiction leads to increased craving and to a decrease in satisfaction. Whereas fulfilment of your heart's desire brings lasting joy.'

Sunday 18 June 2006
Standing on Glastonbury Tor recently, I was instructed to cast a spell.

'Remember,' said my faerie teacher, 'that way back in the far past, the Island of Britain was thickly wooded? In Faerie, those forests still exist. The land holds that memory and up from the land comes a green mist, the exhalation of all those trees, and their leaf light. A green mist is all around you. It is from Faerie and holds the magic of those trees and of the enchantments created by the Fae to increase magic.

'Breathe in the green mist and the leaf light until you are filled with them through and through and are no longer aware of *you* as a part of the everyday World. Now you are at one with the power of Faerie. Feel it renewing your strength, healing you.

'When you are ready, begin to breathe the green mist and leaf light back into your own living World. Turn on the spot so you may breathe it out in every direction. (Do this easily, gently; it isn't hard.) See it, in your mind's eye, spreading out across all the land, healing the human relationship with the countryside, the many types of creature, the rivers, the trees. A green mist, renewing harmony.

'Say something like this: "In the name of the Faerie Queen, may humankind be at one with the land, in good health, in good fortune and in prosperity; at one with the land, to the benefit also of the creatures and plants, the winds and the waters, the deep, rich soil and the tribes of Faerie. So May This Be".'

I tried this at once – and it felt good! Of course, I know that I cannot, all by myself, heal everything and everyone – however many spells of this fey type I manage to do. But every little bit of healing helps. And there are times when even a very small contribution can be enough to tip the balance towards renewed harmony. The equivalent of a magical feather or leaf upon the scales can be just what is needed. (I think it is easy to forget that real change is brought about by many, many people who each do their own small bit towards it.)

Afterwards, I went home on the bus through the Somerset countryside. There were buttercups in the fields and beneath the trees of the apple orchards. Small woods on the hills were a deep, deep green. We passed what looked like somebody's garage with a rose bush growing out of the roof (what was happening there, I wondered?) and the Mendip stone walls were a little tumbled down but still able to keep their boundaries in line. There was a golden glow from the evening sun over everything. It was as if I were looking at life through a bottle of mead, but without the hangover to look forward to.

When I am an old lady, a much older lady than now, I hope that I will still remember that I have had days like this.

Monday 7 December 2009

Such bad news on the radio all the time. If we listen to that too much we could all be driven mad. And most of it isn't even especially accurate. Nor is it necessarily about the most important issues.

I asked my faerie teacher to inspire me with a heart-healing spell, one to renew my courage, which is faltering just now. She muttered to herself about change and loss and about renewal. And then I heard her quietly singing the words to a Faerie spell for heart healing:

A hearth was mine that now is known
by family but not my own.
A time was mine when young and free
I grew as girl from infancy.
The child I was is now long gone.
She is not here in blood or bone.
While bones of those I used to be
in other lives are gone from me
and rest in clay or cave of stone
or at the bottom of the sea.
I change my face, my mind, my song.
My being is as great, as long
as time is wide and deep and high.

For I am always more than I.
A dancer round about the Tree,
there is a Spirit dancing me
(and you and they and he and she)
who casts a spell of travelling
that we may learn how we may sing
in every place to restore grace.

Let this be joy enough to turn
a heart that's cold as pit of stone,
in pain from all the harm we're given
by cruel power, to a hearth fire.

Thursday 10 June 2010
I am at Kilver Court Garden. This is a haunted place. It is
haunted by its own history and this enhances it. For me,
the haunting is personal because my younger self is one of
the ghosts here. I travelled when I was fifteen, with my
family and some friends, on the last train to go to and
from Bournemouth – from Green Park Station in Bath.
That line (the Somerset and Dorset) is long since closed,
but when the trains reached Shepton Mallet, they used to
travel over a viaduct that runs through Kilver Court
Garden. Now, aged fifty-nine, I sit beneath an arch of that
same viaduct, on an old plank propped up on bricks.
(This is an out-of-the-way corner of the garden; the rest
of it has flowers, trees and well-kept lawns in abundance;
even a lake with an island.) In another band of time, my
fifteen-year-old self is still on that train on the viaduct
above. I know that in a few more years she will have dedicated her life to a quest for faerie healing magic. And then
will have turned aside from that quest for a while to try
(rather pointlessly) to become more like a rational and
intellectually sophisticated adult woman (in the eyes of

those who are not fey, that is). It is better to be who we really are, is it not, than to try to be somebody else, some other type? On the other hand, mistakes are a part of being alive. It is all experience. And I would not have wanted to miss any of it. I mentally wave to her up there, my much younger self. And I wonder what she would have thought of me, down here.

In another time, much, much further back, the Romans are still tramping north on the nearby Fosse Way . . . sometimes stopping to trade with the native British, who have set up shop all along the route.

Coming back nearer in time, there is the swirl and roar of an angry crowd; then the leap of flame as workers at Kilver Court Mill torch the place in protest against their working conditions in a past century.

There are many ghosts here, both human and crea-turely. Also, there are ghosts of trees. They are not true ghosts for they are not earthbound, even though they are dead. That is, they do not linger here in our World, largely unseen, but have gone to the Otherworld. Most of them, that is. I am using the word 'ghost' incorrectly. It is just that for me this place is haunted by its own history.

Now, in the present, a squirrel runs straight across the lawn, visitors stroll on the paths, and the small river Sheppey pours into the lake while the gardeners go on attending to beauty so that our souls may be recharged. It is the present that counts most because it is where we are. And yet the present includes the past. The garden's history is so much a part of it right now.

All these 'hauntings' that I have described (and many more) are a part of the garden's ongoing present – and of its future, too.

Tuesday 3 May 2011

I was shown this vision by my faerie teacher.

In a woodland clearing there is a huge tree. It is entirely made out of golden light or fire. But I can also see flickers of green, shaped like leaves, and swaying brown branches and a lichen-covered trunk. These seem to solidify from the gold somehow. This is both a tree of golden fire and, at the same time, a living tree. My teacher now tells me that I am seeing the tree's actual spirit (its energy pattern) as well as its body.

This could be almost any actual tree, almost anywhere. It is also a symbol – the World Tree, a kind of universal axis.

Every separate being of any species, all the creatures and plants and all places with their hills and valleys, their stones and pools, their skies and seas, exist around this Tree, the World Tree. The Fae are at the roots of it. The dead in their ancestral realms are underneath, too. They are beneath the ground, having gone through portals where the land is thinly draped and is much more frail than you might expect. Just as thin and frail as the skeleton of a dead leaf – but concealing a golden light. (Such portals can appear anywhere – the scene of a car crash, for example – and then disappear.) Above, among the branches, there are the stars. This is the realm of the elves of light, those more commonly known as angels. It is also the dwelling of enlightened spirits – the wise and the just – who have attained to a constant harmony by their efforts to learn and grow.

'Notice,' says my faerie teacher, 'how these seemingly separate realms are of one World. The night sky with its stars, the life all around any tree and the land under the tree are all in one World in the land of your everyday reality. Likewise, in the Otherworld, the three realms of land, under land and up in the stars, are really just different aspects of one World.

'All time is present around the Tree. The past, present and future are all equally reachable for those who know how to go to them. All previous lives are there – together with the various possibilities for many lives to come. Here, too, is each dream and aspiration of anyone, together with every memory in Creation. Not all of these are kindly or wholesome, and some are brutal and sick. Around the World Tree, anything is possible. And so it is up to each one of us to gain wisdom and to dream lovingly . . . to learn to make the right choices.'

I look down at my own body. I, too, am made out of golden light as well as flesh and blood.

I look at this sacred unity of all, shown to me in a vision given by Faerie. Just for this moment, there is no more to say.

Wednesday 13 July 2011

At times, I stand on a busy street aghast at the needs I can feel in so many people – the unmet needs for peace and profundity. And I catch glimpses of ghouls and hear their voices, suggesting to the people that all their needs can be assuaged by purchasing something new: a new dress, car, mobile phone . . . something, anything, everything.

I feel like a stranger in a strange land. Don't get me wrong: I, too, love to buy new clothes. Like the Fae with whom I am allied, I love good times and pretty things. But I wonder what we can do to change this unappeased feeling that so many people have. Banishing some of these ghouls would be a start. But more than that, we need to find a way to a fulfilled inner life and sense of meaning for everyone, through a creative spirituality that is free of dogma and is benign, not moralistic. I find this in today's

Paganism; others may find it in the Quaker Church, or in Spiritualism, or (I am certain) in many other beliefs. This creative, experimental spirituality might perhaps be grounded in humanism and – very sorry, but I am English – in moderation?

Saturday 11 June 2011
On Monday, Ashley and I went to Mum's house at Marshfield. Had a most peaceful, nourishing family day. Now an image stays with me of my daughter Emily walking down Marshfield High Street towards her car. Her black clothes waft about her like the wings of many dark butterflies. She is both solidly a woman in the prime of life and a spirit presence of flare and mystery.

Friday 17 June 2011
A phone conversation with my Mum in which she told me that she had spent the afternoon in the park in Chippenham, beside the river Avon. There she had fed the ducks and swans while a pigeon had perched on her shoulder. Then, when she had sat down on a bench, a swan had got up and shared it with her, sitting peacefully in the sun – two fellow beings in tranquil ease.

I see all this with my mind's eye. Eighty-two years old, bright-eyed and feeding a great horde of birds at the water's edge. Birds that I imagine approaching her like creatures from a Grimm's fairy tale; somehow taking from her outstretched hand a blessing as well as bread.

Wednesday 1 February 2012
Ideally . . . I am in a state of communion with the land's beauty and good faerie presences. I travel into the Otherworld in spirit without any effort. This all happens

as spontaneously as a dream but I am awake.

I shift my shape into the form of a tree and I am also a bird in one of the branches, and I am most truly me. I am singing with a faerie voice and the song comes from the bird's throat. It is the song of a wren, and it is wordless and yet conveys a spell that wells up in me from the land. This brings harmonious balance to all species. It increases the trees, bees, butterflies, birds, native fishes, wildflowers and all threatened wild creatures. It purifies the waters and cleanses the breeze; renews the goodness of the soil, itself; renews harmony between humankind and the rest of Nature. This joyful song is what I am for in each of the Worlds. It is not my song. It is that of the Faerie Queen and, ultimately, of Mother Earth. I am simply one of her mediums. It has the same effect as the faerie dancing, which I have seen sometimes in visions: the faerie dancers in their white dresses patched and pied with black, the harlequin dancers. Their smallest gesture helps to keep the seas in balance with the land, the rocks with starlight, the seabirds flying. I see them perform arabesques in slow motion. They do not dance in chorus. Each one has her own concerns and moves as her own magic dictates. With one slowly raised arm and a pointing finger, any one of these Valkyries can transform any cause of harm into something creative, or return it to its rightful place so that no harm is done. They are in complete resonance with any place where they dance. They have become the mediums for great Nature Herself, in all Her transformative, evolutionary power and Her drive towards ever-changing manifestation – life itself.

This is what I would like to become one day after I am dead: something like these dancers, but with sound and in poetry.

SEVEN

THE ANCESTORS

The easiest way for most of us to relate to the Otherworld is via contact of a private, spontaneous kind with our own beloved dead – our deceased relatives, lovers or friends. We can reach out to them – or rather *in* – from inside ourselves. We can talk to them in our hearts: sometimes with passionate requests for help; sometimes with raw grief and love; sometimes to pass on family news about, for example, the birth of a child. Rationally, most present-day people do not *believe* that the dead can hear us, or at least sense that we are thinking about them. But in our hearts we continue to speak to them because the heart knows differently.

The dead can speak to us; and they may have a great deal more influence upon our lives than most people believe. Although they are in the Otherworld, they may still have strong feelings of love and concern for those they have left behind, may still affect us with their good wishes and with the blessings they send to our present-day selves, may still continue to shape our living World.

In spite of the message of horror movies, the dead's influence is rarely sinister – for why should it be? They are our forebears, our kin and friends. They will help us in any way that they can, most often by guiding messages that may be heard inside our minds, or even (occasionally) as actual words spoken externally and out loud. But the dead cannot make us do things – not even for our own good (and certainly not for our destruction). That is why, in the rare event of an ill-wishing by one of them, we are unlikely to be affected unless, that is, we collude with them by secretly wishing our own undoing for reasons of some kind of guilt, perhaps. Relationships with the dead are much like those with the living in that they are a two-way trans-action. In other words, we can always choose our own response to any message or wish. Fear is never appropriate because we have as much power in respect of the dead as when they were living. In physical terms, we have more than they do. And, therefore, if their power rested in phys-ical dominance while they were alive – well, they have lost that here in the Living World. They do still have psychic or subtle power – but then, so do we! And theirs will not have been increased merely by the fact that they are dead. In any case, the dead whom we have loved will never be dangerous.

In my family, there is a story about my great-grandfa-ther's attitude to his dead wife. It seems that after she had died, he announced his intention of spending that night in the same bed with her. His daughter, my grandmother, was horrified.

'Surely that would be terrifying,' she said, 'even though she's my Mum? All night with a dead person?'

'Why should 1 be frightened?' he answered. 'Your Mum never hurt me when she was alive so why should she want to now that she's dead?' And he went ahead and did just what he had said he wanted to do.

I find this Heathcliff-like behaviour of an old man very

moving. It is not what everyone would want to do – especially not these days when we are so much more removed from primal reality (or think we are) and so much more squeamish. But whatever my great-grandfather still had to fear, it certainly was not from his dead wife, as he pointed out. He outlived her by eleven years and I am sure their reunion in the Otherworld was joyful.

Other things as well as love can make a link go on. In fact, the Celts believed this so strongly that it is said they would lend money to a friend on the understanding that it could be paid back in another life.

Reincarnation seems to be no barrier to our living connection with the dead. That is, a person may be reborn in another place and time and yet still be contactable as our ancestor or dead friend or partner within the Otherworld. This defies all logic, obviously, but the experience of some psychics, including myself, indicates that it may be so. An atom, as is known to quantum physicists, can be in many different places at once. So it might not be beyond belief that we can do the same thing. An individual spirit may have had many incarnations, each one of them still living in the Otherworld as an ancestral spirit, even while the latest life is happening right here. Certainly, in the Faerie tradition, it is taught that a part of each of our souls remains in the Otherworld while we are living. This is our Otherworldly counterpart, sometimes known as the 'fetch' or 'co-walker'. It seems that each person we become in our perhaps countless incarnations has his or her own co-walker (or whatever it is that remains in Faerie), each one containing a part of the essential self, the spirit. In other words, each one is a different version of just one person – or something like that. Living in the Age of Quantum Physics has made it more possible for our minds to accept this kind of vision. And yet it has been implied, or at least compatible, all along in terms of some psychic experience and some faerie lore.

If, as Faerie traditions and the poet T.S. Elliot have said, all time is eternally present, then we could each be living many lives at once in both this and the Otherworld. This makes sense of the idea of a multiplicity of souls, each one belonging to the same spirit. Ultimately, of course, we are each avatars of the Spirit of Earth, in one form or another, we who live here. Each one of us and our co-walkers are manifestations of one Spirit, that of the Earth, in human form. I find that ideas like this for me make plausible the possibility that each one of us has many souls and many forms, some incarnate here (in different time-bands), and some there, in the Otherworld. And that, therefore, we can talk to our dead as the people we knew even if they have long since begun other lives as other people.

None of this is a fixed ideology. You cannot have one in realms of Mystery where paradox and trans-rational facts entirely hold sway. No one can ever (rationally) know the certain truth, and there will always be some things that our minds just cannot grasp. Our minds cannot grasp quantum physics, either. Some of the laws that have been discovered sound entirely impossible on any logical basis, but they are still viable. This does not, of course, mean that all irrational theories are true, most definitely not. It does mean that if you think like a mystic (in other words, think like a fey) or like a poet, you may sense the truth. So I shall go on chatting to my beloved Dad, even though he died back in 1979.

Well, to get back to our theme of connections with the dead, there are many kinds. For one thing, there can be links of hate. These, too, can persist after death, especially in the case of ghosts who feel they have grounds for resentment and bitterness. But we are not powerless in these cases. Just as in this World, we can decide to turn away. If we decide a relationship must come to an end, then sooner or later, it definitely will. If the dead person does not seem to give up and continues to obsess us, we can call confidently on Otherworldly help. For example, we can call on the Faerie King. As a British Pagan, I would probably name him as Gwyn ap Nudd. He has many names, but I like that one. It means 'Light, son of Night'. Or I might call on the Swan Maidens, those faerie women who take the dead to the Otherworld to be purified and transformed. Another name for these is 'Valkyries' and they can appear in the guise of ravens rather than swans. Nor do they only take dead warriors up to Heaven, as is suggested in Norse mythology. As Lynda Welch tells us in her book *Goddess of the North*, they can also heal a wounded soul. I would call upon them, or upon Gwyn ap Nudd, to take away any troublesome ghost to be purified and healed so that he or she might come into new harmony and give up their hatred.

No doubt, there are equivalent figures in each of the World's traditions and faiths. Christians sometimes call upon St Michael for help in these situations. If you are on the Faerie Path and do not yet know any specific names with which you feel comfortable, it is enough to call out from within yourself to the Great Queen of Faerie, who is the Mother of the Fae and Lady of all the dead, everywhere and in all time. Ask her in your own words to send help and protection. She never fails to answer if called upon sincerely and urgently. In any case, I would like to stress that there is never any need to be terrified of ghosts. Help is always available from the Otherworld if we ask for it. As with the living, they are only people. However angry or misguided, usually they need to be heard or helped or reassured.

In his book *British Goblins* the nineteenth-century

author Wirt Sikes tells us that the usual way to be rid of a ghost is to ask what it wants. Sometimes the answer might be to retrieve money (or other belongings) that the person had hidden while living; often the ghost might insist that the item should be given to a named person. But sometimes the ghost might prefer that the money should just be thrown into a river or open water. Other ghostly requests might tend to be for intangible things such as forgiveness – always from a named person towards whom the ghost felt some guilt.

In Pagan Europe and in the rest of the World, so far as I know, people were expected to pay serious attention to the dead. They regularly gave offerings of food and drink. These were put out at burial mounds, or in a shrine at the family home, or in other places of relevance, such as the fields in which the dead person had worked. In some places, this custom still continues up to the present day. Even now, there are British households in which food is set out for dead family members. This usually means that a place is set for them at the table and they are served with a meal that includes some of their favourite food and drink. That meal is left on the table overnight, even though any plates or mugs used by the living have been cleared up. The traditional name for this offering is 'the dumb supper'. It is sometimes given on the anniversary of a person's death or on what used to be their birthday, but the commonest time to do it is on Hallowe'en. This is because it is the old European Day of the Dead – the traditional Celtic festival of Samhain – and, therefore, known to be a time when, as the witches say, the 'veil' that hides this World from the Otherworld is very thin. Naturally, it is on this day that many present-day Pagans commune with the dead, and send them love and blessings and ask their advice.

Fey people may be inclined to put out food and drink

for the dead, or for the visiting Fae at any time that it feels appropriate, such as at the new or full moon, or just on any day if they sense that they have Otherworldly guests present.

The idea is that the dead person or visiting Fae can be offered hospitality here in our World. Some people like to light a candle for the returning dead, the better to show them the way to their former home and to welcome them. This is a very lovely and potent thing to do, stretching back as it does through many hundreds of years when a light left burning was often a sign to a living traveller making their tired way through a dark night.

When we remember that in faerie lore anything in our World may have an Otherworldly counterpart, it is easy to see how this works. The light, partly ensouled by our own intention that it should be a loving gift, can be seen by the dead. They do not see *everything* because it is not given to them to do so. Their realm is not the same part of the Otherworld in which our co-walkers dwell while we are alive. But there can be a breakthrough, or perhaps a merging of the dimensions when the powerful magic of what we call love requires this to be so.

It should go without saying that no candle should be left unattended on a window sill if there could be a risk of fire from billowing curtains or the activities of a pet or from any other cause.

In the Roman Catholic Church, there is still a tradition of spiritual work being done for the dead. There is the requiem Mass as well as the more personal practice of lighting candles for the dead and of saying prayers for their well-being. All of this has roots in the European Pagan traditions in which the dead were not necessarily seen as having reached an involuntary, static condition in either Heaven or Hell, but as continuing their quest for personal and spiritual harmony through other lives and in other forms in this or the Otherworld. The dead were also seen as continuing to care for their descendants and as still having power and influence. Some of these ideas are enshrined or implied in Spiritualism, where contact with the dead is perceived as being respectful and also helpful, provided that we do not make too many demands upon them, but instead let them be with us when they are able without compromising their own Otherworldly progress. (In any healthy tradition, Faerie or otherwise, we are advised to honour the dead and to value their continuing love but also – at the same time – to let them go.)

It is said that the dead (or the Fae) can take the subtle essence of any food or drink that is given to them, but it should be composted or buried the next day even if it appears completely untouched. Be that as it may, it decays very soon after burying or composting. There is an old belief that it brings very bad luck if we eat or drink anything that has been offered to the Otherword. Much safer to bury it! Then those in the Otherworld can consume it, but those of this World cannot.

All such practices are symbolic/magical matters and they are very ancient indeed in one form or another. In some parts of the World and at some points in history, they are said to have been connected with a need to appease the dead, to somehow make it up to them for no longer being alive. In other places or at other times, it was more of a way to maintain the connection and perhaps to remind the dead that we still value being blessed by them, and to show love and respect. Magically, it was also linked with the idea that the life force in food – and particularly in meat – can be given to the dead or the Fae to strengthen them in their actions here when we want to ask them for help. This was one reason for the appalling practice of blood sacrifice.

But not the only reason. During the Iron Age, in particular, here in Britain as well as in other countries in Europe, men were killed in order that they might negotiate with Otherworldly powers on behalf of their own tribe or people – their living people. Being chosen as such a sacrifice is said to have been a great honour for which only the best from among the young men were chosen. It is also said that they went to their deaths willingly, but who knows? These Sacred Kings (or, occasionally, Queens) were contactable by the living. They could be prayed to for help. The Christian idea of Jesus as having 'died for his people' and as interceding for them with God is much the same when you come down to the bare bones of the story.

In earlier tribal practices, it seems to have been the bones of the dead, which were used in magical rites to commune with them and to gain their guidance and help. These were sometimes the bones of the already dead, for at this stage, comparatively few were sacrifices. (If you would like an account of how and why these rites employed by the Neolithic British became an Iron Age nightmare of head-hunting and terror, I know of no better book than John Grigsby's *Warriors of the Wasteland*.) And it seems to me that there are as many ways to refine or to degrade our links with the dead as there are human types and motivations. It is also obvious that human sacrifice is still practised, though nowadays for money and less openly as a result of toxic industries, warfare, and the unfair distribution of this World's resources, among other things. So we still do not seem to have had enough experience as a species to have gained the wisdom to prevent such ruthlessness. (*How long does it take, I wonder?*) And we still seem to think, or mainstream culture would have us believe, that communication with the dead is either impossible or a fraught and dangerous undertaking and should be avoided.

And all the while, how near the dead really are for each one of us! My heart often senses them. They are here in the gaps between one heartbeat and the next. And they seem to co-exist with the very young, those who are still in that border state of consciousness, the liminal, unexplained and deeply known. They are certainly at one with the unborn, those who have not yet even been conceived.

Saturday 24 October 2015

It is now almost Samhain, the old Celtic Festival of the Dead, still celebrated on 31 October each year by witches and Druids and by modern Pagans of many kinds. In Mexico, the Festival of the Dead is held on this day. The Church of England honours the dead on 1 and 2 November, days which the Church calls the Feast of All Saints and the Feast of All Souls. In Britain, we also remember the dead of two World Wars on a date very close to Samhain, the Sunday nearest to 11 November: 'Poppy Day' or 'Remembrance Sunday' is the nearest we now come to a publicly celebrated, communal Day of the Dead.

In all the different lands and eras of this World, people have probably set aside a special time to remember the dead. It is natural that most people prefer to remember their own dead, which often means their own dead parents or grandparents. But the Chinese also have a traditional day of remembrance for those who died without leaving any descendants. In China, you are still celebrated as an ancestor, even if you did not have any children of your own and have no living relatives left to honour you.

We are all future ancestors or ancestresses, whether we are lucky enough to have descendants or not. Our contributions to life and our psychic presence within the Soul of the Land have the potential to influence future generations long after we are gone. For childless writers and artists or for anyone in the public eye this may seem rather obvious. But a life of quiet kindness or of constructive effort will also bear fruit long after the person has been forgotten. For example, the campaigner who gains better health care for children or the welfare worker who always treats people fairly and goes the extra mile to help people gain the benefits to which they are entitled, these leave a healthier, more harmonious World behind them. Their legacy to life is not children, but other, less tangible things. The farmer who tends his acres well will leave behind healthy land so that in future people can grow good food there. One way and another, each and every being is an ancestor or ancestress. This includes all species, for ancient trees and creatures were the forebears of the land we know now. So we can and should celebrate the 'landcestors' as they are sometimes called as well as the human dead.

As a fey person, I am aware of the dead more often than once a year at Samhain; most of all, I am aware of my Dad. There have been frequent periods in which I have felt in contact with him (briefly) day after day. Usually, this has felt as though it were initiated by him from the Otherworld rather than by myself from this living World. I may be doing nothing special when it happens – just day-dreaming or waiting for a train or sitting in the garden – and suddenly he appears to my inner sight. Often, he indicates some upcoming event, whether happy or sad, beneficial or dangerous. (His predictions have always proved to be accurate.) He himself had fey abilities when he was alive.

A Blessing for the Dead

Switch off all phones and sit somewhere quiet where you will not be interrupted. Have a candle and matches ready. Think of the Source of All Life, the Great Mother, in Her guise of the Great Queen of Faerie who brings change and then renewal to all beings that die. And remember the dead whom you have loved as being in Her care. This is another way of saying that they are now at one with the Spirit that runs through everything within the Otherworld – or at one with Mother Earth, but within Nature's other dimension.

When you feel relaxed and your mind is focused towards Faerie rather than towards the World we live in, say something like this:

'I light this candle for [*here name your dead loved one/s*]. May [*he/she/they*] be blessed now and always with [*here name three things you wish for them, such as happiness, good fortune and peace*].'

Continue: 'In the name/s of [*here name the Power/s you hold most sacred – for example, the Great Mother and Great Father, or the Source of Life, or the Goddess and God or Lady and Lord of the Realm of Faerie*], wherever [*he/she/they*] now reside and wherever [*he/she/they*] may go, by starlight, earthlight and sunlight, so may this be.'

Leave the candle to burn down while you go and do other things – unless you need to go out or go to sleep, in which case extinguish it, and re-light it when you can.

If you want to bless the dead (or a Faerie familiar spirit; indeed, anyone in the Otherworld) while you are outside, you need not bother with a candle. Instead, you can pour some spring water onto the ground for them. The water should be from a local spring or, failing that, from a local tap; don't use shop-bought water in a plastic bottle that has been shipped or flown in from far away. If you have no water with you, just go ahead without it for the real offering is the blessing itself; the flame and water are extra things.

Touch the land while you say the blessing. If you are uncomfortable squatting down or kneeling, then you may touch a tree since its roots go down into the earth.

The dead have all gone into the land as far as their mortal remains are concerned. Even after a cremation, the ashes will usually be interred or scattered somewhere. Their souls are within the Soul of the Land – that is to say, the Soul of Nature. So the land links us all, both living and dead. Just touch the ground somewhere tranquil such as a garden, hill-top or nature reserve. You can say the blessing inside your mind rather than out loud if there are people close by and you wish to be completely private. It is as easy as prayer and just as immediate.

Wednesday 20 May 2015
Lizzie is awakened about 2.00 a.m. by a woman weeping. It is the sound of utter despair, quite dreadful to hear, a shattering and terrifying grief. Lizzie cannot listen.

It is coming out of the darkness in her own house, as disturbing as any single thing she has ever heard in her life. She is not dreaming – this has woken her out of deep sleep and now she is awake it goes on and on. She lies wishing for it to stop with every part of her being.

Is it the cry of the banshee (the *bean sidhe*), the faerie woman whose cry, according to folklore, foretells a coming death? Her familiar spirit – a welcome companion in such circumstances – explains that it is not.

'It comes from someone in your own World in the past. You are hearing something that happened, but it is not a haunting. There is no unquiet, earthbound spirit here. It is just that your old house has held many griefs in its time and sometimes the fey, such as yourself, can experience the past or the future of a place as well as the present.'

Lizzie happens to know that a woman who used to live in her house lost a son in a road accident, an eight-year-old. Is it she who is crying? Her faerie familiar confirms that it is. It was all a long time ago but somewhere within the ever-present cycles of time it is also now.

Just as the grief has reached forward, Lizzie reaches back in time and tries to send comfort. She does this by her empathy with the grieving woman, so that heart to heart, she can send love and compassion. She knows it is possible because, beyond time and beyond words, we are all one – as her familiar has taught her. But it is oddly difficult because of the terrible tearing sound of the grief. Lizzie cannot concentrate.

The next day, she succeeds. She lights a candle for the grieving woman and says these words:

'May there be love and comfort for you, dear soul, from the Great Ancestress of us all, the Great Mother. May there be healing spirits around you in Her name. May your grief be soothed and your heart healed. May you know in your heart that no link of love is ever broken. All the mothers and fathers who have ever lived and lost a child are with you now. They are strengthening you.'

And back in 1951, the grieving woman lifts her head. Her heart feels a little bit less heavy for no reason she can explain.

CHAPTER EIGHT

THE FAERIE FUNERAL

To recapitulate (a little), in the Faerie Tradition the souls of the living are seen as existing not only within Nature but within another, more subtle dimension of it, one that is quite close to the everyday World. And after death, we go on existing in this same realm, this more inward aspect, aware to some extent of this living World but no longer of it. Those who by choice or by accident remain in that condition, that place, are known as 'earthbound'. They are ghosts. Most of us go on much further, travel right through into the Otherworld completely, fully conscious there rather than here. This change is experienced as a passage through a tunnel into light, or as a voyage across water, or as some kind of winged flight, according to most of the World's oldest known beliefs and also according to some who have had a Near Death Experience (NDE) and according to those who have studied what has been said by people about their former incarnations, right up to and after a previous death.

Having made the full transition, we find ourselves in a part of the place that used to be called the Realm of

Faerie – and still is, to some of us. This is a dimension that could be called the Soul of Nature. It is not only ruled by the Great Queen of Faerie, it is the Great Queen of Faerie. The land is Her being; She is the greater Soul in which our souls exist. (A difficult concept for people reared in the belief that we each exist in a kind of bubble cut off from everything else – rather than being continuous with and a part of everything else.)

Beyond and deep within the Realm of Soul is the Realm of Spirit, that which is energy, pattern and archetype and which brings joy, healing and harmony. This is both deep down at the healing heart of Faerie (where it is sometimes seen as being a great sea of golden light) and is also reachable through Faerie skies, high up in a place of radiant beauty to which some of the dead are taken by winged spirits or birds. Clearly, these form the basis for later ideas of Heaven and Hell – Heaven being the realm of harmony high above, and Hell being the bad place below. Yet there is nothing I know of in Faerie lore about eternal torture by fiery demons. (A Christian friend has told me that there seems to have been nothing of this in early Christianity, either.) In fact, the Faerie Queen's great sea of golden light or her cauldron of flames are said to bring renewal and a deep sense of joyful communion – happiness.

Many people, including (so far as I know) the early Christians, believe (or have believed at an earlier point in their history) that we each have many lives in this World so we can evolve enough to live 'above' in the heavenly realm, whether that is seen literally or interpreted as an ascension to a finer dimension of Nature. The Celts certainly believed this, as did the ancient Egyptians. Beyond that we cannot go if looking for any kind of consensus because there are many cultural differences over beliefs about how many dimensions there are in the

Otherworld and who lives there and so forth. Besides, as my faerie teacher has said, in either World we have only a partial and limited view of reality because we cannot rationalize what essentially is and always will be Mystery. When we are trying to fit everything into some kind of fixed system, we need to remember that rational concepts can only take us so far. She tells me our intuitions about these things can be more reliable (providing they are not tainted by any dogma or preconceptions). She urges me to say that we should each value our own 'psychic poetry' about the Otherworld. This does not have to be written down – indeed, it is sometimes beyond us to do so. But it lives inside each one of us, and an intense experience such as bereavement can often release it, bringing it into our conscious minds.

It is of inestimable value.

Fey people have such intuitions, whether bereaved or not, and may know instinctively how to communicate with the dead or with faerie presences of other species than humankind. If not, they will certainly feel the soul's reality in life and death and sense the Soul of Nature when they see beauty in *this* World. They may also know how to construct a funeral rite for someone, based on the old faerie traditions.

In Northern Europe the powers of Nature that take a soul to the Otherworld when a person has died have been called the Wild Hunt. Tradition says that they ride out during the winter season, beginning at the old Celtic festival of Samhain, to find and gather up all those among the dead who have not yet made the full transition into the Otherworld, those souls who linger on in the places they loved within this World. The work of the Wild Hunt is necessary because a soul who is 'earthbound' (a ghost) is often unable to move on completely and can be very confused and unhappy. (The percentage of those who are malevolent is very small in contrast to the number of those who are simply lost and unaware of how to move on.) They are not at all like those souls I mentioned earlier who have made the full transition and yet come to 'visit' now and again, appearing in a vision to give us advice or well-wishes.

Many ghosts really need the help of living psychic healers, or witches or spiritualists, for they often make strenuous efforts to hide until the Wild Hunt has passed them by.

The Hunt is believed to be led by a God of the Earth (an alternative name for a Faerie King). He is known in Britain by many names: Wild Edric; Gwyn ap Nudd; Herne the Hunter. In France, he has been called Le Grand Veneur; in Germany, Hans Von Hackelnberg. The Iroquois people of North America know of a similar hunter of lost souls they call Heno the Thunder.

In other versions of this tradition, the hunters may be huntresses and they can be winged or web-footed. These are led by a Goddess of Earth (a Faerie Queen) who has been known in Europe by many names including: Dame Holda; Frau Goden; Habondia; Herodias; Percht; and, more earthily, Bertha Goosefoot. In the Norse tradition, these huntresses are known as 'Valkyries' and are led by Vala, the Queen of Fate, or by Freya, whose name means 'the Lady'.

In indigenous traditions from all over the World, there is also a tale of a spirit bird who is, or who represents, the Goddess or God who takes the dead to the Otherworld. Sometimes, these bird-spirit stories are linked to the constellation Cygnus, the name of which means 'swan', and are believed to show the deceased person being taken to or towards that part of the sky. Yet the bird can often be raven or eagle, crow, or even vulture, depending upon the part of the World from which the story originates. This may be a poetic metaphor, showing the dead ascending to a finer, less dense dimension than this we inhabit while we are living; also, it may be a perception of those who help the dead – winged beings, Pagan angels, shape-shifters who can become birds or women and by whom a soul is borne upwards.

The bird-spirit is also an image that could relate to burial customs from our Pagan past. For example, there was a practice in Britain called 'Burial in Air'. In this, the dead person was put on a high platform, well away from their village and too high up for the living to see them. They were then left until the carrion birds such as crows or ravens had picked their bones clean. It may have been thought that this brought the soul a swift release and successful journey into the Otherworld. Among Arctic peoples, the soul has been seen as a seed carried in the bird-spirit's beak, to be taken into the land and buried so that the person may be reborn in their tribe as a new baby.

Lizzie Webfoot and Johnnie Hoof know about this kind of thing. They may not know much academically, but give them one or two key images and they can feel how these work in their bones. They know it in their hearts and souls, and can each honour their own dead with simple rites for them, based on ideas of journeying by air or water.

My husband's mother died at the Winter Solstice in 2013 and we held a Faerie funeral for her. She was a practising Christian and a sincere one, but she also had a respect for our beliefs and the Faerie path. Indeed, she was one of those pure souls who are at one with their mainstream spiritual tradition and yet comfortable with other peoples' beliefs and choices. In other words, she was not fundamentalist. Like ourselves, she was far less impressed by any religious label a person might wear than in whether they tried to act kindly and live with integrity.

This lovely person (her name was Barbara) chose the

hymns and readings for her own Christian funeral quite a long while before she died. And so, in due course we went to Church for the rite she had wanted and helped to plan. But there was a long delay, rather more than a month, before this took place. As fey people who each loved her, we were then faced with a difficult decision. More than a month was to go by between her death and her funeral, a whole cycle of the Moon and more, with no rites for the passing of this very special lady. This was a huge emotional strain and also it just felt plain wrong. What, if anything, should we do about it?

The January days ground by in grief and tension. Finally, we could bear it no longer. After consulting with the faerie spirits who guide us and with our own deepest feelings, we gave her a Faerie funeral to precede (though not to replace) the more formal one of her own tradition. We based the funeral on ideas and beliefs from British indigenous traditions as found in folk and faerie lore. In no sense were we trying to recreate what our British ancestors may have done in the Bronze Age or whenever. We are firmly convinced that today's rites must fit easily with today's culture and way of life. Ancient beliefs and magical knowledge are our heritage and to be respected, but we should feel free to reinterpret them in ways that speak to us now. And that is what we lovingly tried to do.

THE FAERIE FUNERAL
For Barbara Elizabeth,
who died 22 December 2013, aged 90 years

We did this by candlelight in our own home. Of course, there was no coffin and no congregation. Except for the faerie presences who thronged the room, we were alone with Barbara's spirit.

RAE   This is the faerie rite for Barbara Elizabeth, beloved mother of Ashley, Jill and Annette, beloved friend of many. By love, may her soul be blessed on this and each day and night, wherever she may now go.

ASHLEY We light this candle to brighten my mother's path to the Otherworld. Let it shine back in time to her moment of death, giving her light whenever she has need of it.
[*He lights the candle*]

RAE   We call to the Great Queen of Faerie. Lady, we know you in the call of ravens and in owl-cry and as the wind in bare trees and the sound of an ebbing tide. Come to us. We invoke the compassionate song on your cold breath; your voice of enchantment that calls to each soul, singing them home to your realm to be made whole again, at one with the Great Soul of Nature yet individual. Arise, Great Queen and bless this rite. Bless Barbara Elizabeth into her rightful place in the Otherworld. Bring her to your bright hall to be welcomed and healed. Let her rejoin her dead family and her many friends and rejoice in freedom.

ASHLEY Hail, Queen of Faerie.

RAE   [*singing*]
Come, gentle Barbara,
Lady of grace.
Come and be welcomed
in your right place.
The birds of the morning
are all flown away.
The Sun is now setting
upon the cold day.

Come with the twilight
within the Hill.
In the wide lands of Faerie
be welcomed, dear soul.

ASHLEY We call now to the Faerie King, he who is Lord of the World in the Hollow Hills, Lord of the Realm of Death and the Ways between This and the Otherworld. Guardian and Guide of Souls, I ask you to bring my mother, Barbara, into the Realm of Faerie, right into the Faerie Queen's company, just as I tell her tale. May it be as I speak. First, as the boatman upon the tide that bears her away from this World's bone-strewn shore, following the dead who have gone before, Great Lord, you bring her to an island: within a beach cave that is dark and cold, you lead her through a Faerie door and into a dim passage; and now she steps along both nervous and brave but within your care – steps into radiant golden light to reunite with those she loves among the dead. And you are with her still and lead her in joy, made youthful again, to dance in a Faerie ring. And then send her on her way to meet with those of her own Christian tradition of her free will. Hail, wild Lord of Faerie. Hail, Faerie King.

RAE Wherever you go, Barbara, may you be blessed with good health, good fortune and fulfilment of your best possible destiny. This day, this night and forever more in any of the realms in each of the Worlds, in the names of the Great Mother of Fate – the Faerie Queen – and of the Lord of Light within Darkness – the Faerie King – so may this always be.

ASHLEY   We celebrate your life and spirit.

[*There then follows a description of Barbara's life and her nature, by Ashley, and then by Rae*]

RAE   Great Queen of Faerie, Queen of us all, Lady to whom all return in the Hill when this life is done, we call to you now to send help and comfort to we who are mourning. By twilight and dawn and also at noon, by each of the liminal times and places, let the dead speak to us, now and always, and we to them, re-making links of love in strong connection.

[*There then follows a pause for a time of silence, in which each person communes with Barbara, speaking to her gently within the quiet of their own minds, sensing her presence within the Otherworld and being open to anything she might say or, beyond words, convey*]

ASHLEY   Barbara, beloved mother and friend, our love goes with you till we meet again.
RAE   Thanks to the Faerie Queen and Faerie King and to our kindly familiar spirits from Faerie for blessings on this rite. Hail and farewell to all who attended here.

Well, that is what we did, early one January evening. And we felt that something had been healed by it, for us and for Barbara's spirit. As I said, the rite is actually based on images and teachings from British Faerie lore, but there are similar ideas, sometimes linked with birds and sometimes with boats, in indigenous traditions worldwide.

We knew at the time that we were invoking Faerie

Powers which the dead need to meet soon after death rather than several weeks later. But, as they say of the Otherworld, 'time runs differently there', and we had been guided that our rite would take effect back in time (from our living point of view) when Barbara needed it.

We also knew that the dead usually find their way to the Otherworld, or are found by the Faerie King's representatives and led there, without any rite. So what we did could have been redundant. And yet . . . yet it felt essential that we do *something*, and not entirely for our own emotional reasons. First, we hoped that it was a kind of psychic resolution for Barbara as well as for ourselves in the reorientation of her soul towards the Otherworld while maintaining her sense of communion with this World, should she want that. But most of all, we did it because a formal expression of love and good wishes together with an invocation of Faerie Powers can only be protective of a newly dead person.

Not everyone finds their way through – or, failing that, is found by the Wild Hunt or the Swan Maidens and rescued. If they did all arrive in the Otherworld, then earthbound spirits would not exist. But we know for certain that Barbara will not spend the time between now and her next life 'between the Worlds', earthbound. She has gone to the Otherworld completely. Our minds are at rest on that.

Nor did we think that the rite we performed was incompatible with the Christian funeral that it preceded since all must enter the Otherworld by the ways of Nature, even to meet with spirit presences from the Christian faith or from any other. However, we knew that in life Barbara had approved of our beliefs and magical practices. Had she been a person to whom our Path seemed unacceptable or wrong, we would not have held the Faerie funeral for her.

Instead, we would have waited for the belated Christian funeral, even against our deepest feelings, for the dead are still people, so it seems important to honour *their* feelings and beliefs and not to dismiss their spirituality. It can be a difficult decision. But the vibrant psychic atmosphere of Barbara's faerie funeral and the ease of our spirit communion with her reassured us that she felt comfortable with what we did.

Now the worst of the long work of mourning is over. And still I see her smiling face in visions that come in quiet moments. Like all the dead, she is safe in Nature's other dimension, a place with its own natural laws and areas where the exhausted dead are made whole again once they have rested. And given the chance to take stock of their former lives and to understand how they affected others for good or ill; and shown how to enhance their descendants' lives with blessings. Or so I am told by my faerie teacher and so psychic research and faerie tradition confirm. You may have a sense of these things yourself, if you are fey.

But what do the symbols mean – those images around which we constructed the Faerie funeral? Well, Faerie is said to be reachable in many ways, as we have seen. One is that you may be sung into the Otherworld by (in Welsh tradition) the blackbirds of Rhiannon. Rhiannon is a Welsh Faerie Goddess. So I sang for Barbara, intending thereby to serve the Faerie Queen's purposes. As we have also seen, the shape-shifting qualities of Faerie mean that, blackbird or woman, I could weave enchantments by using sound or song. Indeed, song is a major part of magic that is derived from or linked with faerie, that or poetry, as anyone will know who has studied the Bardic tradition of the Druids.

In our rite there is more than one reference to a place called 'the Hill'. This is because 'The Land within the

Hollow Hills' is an old name for Faerie. It may be a reference to the burial mounds our ancestors made – barrows – or even that hump in the ground you get with a newly-dug grave – small 'hills' in which the dead are laid to rest and which may then be seen as portals through which they enter Faerie. But there is another reason why hills are said to 'contain' the Otherworld.

In Britain, there are hills such as, most famously, Glastonbury Tor, which are entrances into Faerie. The Tor is the abode of the Faerie King, Gwyn ap Nudd, and his realm within it is not confined to the dimensions of the inside of that hill. It holds not only his Court, but an entire country. Other hills exist with similar folk or faerie lore and others again, which are more in the nature of departure points for such places (or which may have been perceived in that way). For example, back in the past when Glastonbury was an island each winter, surrounded by floods on the undrained moors, the idea of the faerie boatman rowing deceased people to the Isle of the Dead would have made sense. That may be why the nearby hill-fort known as Cadbury Castle was found to contain a boat bearing human remains when excavated. The boat was pointing exactly in the direction of Glastonbury Tor so it may have been that some of the dead were buried like that in order that the mythic faerie boatman could ferry them over, once the winter floods had set in. The man in the boat inside Cadbury Castle had lived in the early Bronze Age. As Paul Devereux tells us in his book *Haunted Land*, ghost roads and ghost waterways are found throughout Europe, according to folklore, linking one locale with another. Traditional routes taken by the Wild Hunt do the same thing. (In fact, throughout the World, these ideas seem to have been widespread.)

Scandinavians of the Bronze Age – and later – sent some

of their dead to the Otherworld by ship burials. The Egyptian God Osiris, Lord of the Otherworld, had his mythic 'Boat of Days', while, to the Greeks, the ferryman Charon took the dead across the water. This theme of the dead crossing rivers or seas to reach their destination is widespread. However, we have conflated the figures of Faerie King and Faerie Boatman in our rite which may offend purists, as these figures are normally viewed as separate Beings. But what we did worked for us on that occasion. Perhaps at another time it might seem more right to make a distinction.

Sometimes our ancestors feared the Hollow Hills and the Faerie Boatman, feared also the Faerie Queen and King, seeing them as sinister figures to do with decay and darkness and birds of prey. Indeed, these are the guises and themes by which they and their work can appear to us while we are living, for obvious reasons. In the Otherworld, they can shift shape, becoming benign powers in a place of renewal – or not, depending upon our own inner state. This is shown in the German faerie tale 'Mother Holle', in which a girl who behaves kindly in the Otherworld is blessed with good fortune by the Faerie Queen, while her unkind sister receives bad luck and bad treatment. However, it is in this living World that we journey towards death, hence the use of the term 'bone-strewn', to denote the shores of this World from which my mother-in-law Barbara is borne away. In the Otherworld, we journey to life, for it is the place of regeneration from which we either reincarnate here or take up another existence in that World. The Otherworld then is the place of new life, one way or another.

To the Germanic and Scandinavian peoples of the past, the realm that is 'inside the Hill' could lead to an existence similar to that the dead person had known in life. This theme was used in the BBC television series 'Life on Mars' and in its sequel 'Ashes to Ashes', in which dead detectives try to resolve their own moral, spiritual and psychological issues while continuing to catch criminals. Progress through this realm, which may be the foundation of the Christian idea of Purgatory, could lead to being in another part of the Otherworld, perhaps one of greater harmony linked with or symbolized by the stars. Alternatively, it could lead to a rebirth within the living World. Or, if the soul could not achieve a change of attitude, it could lead to a period of seeming to drift helplessly in a kind of grey mist, or even to being, as it were, recycled completely so that not a trace remains of the original individual.

Naturally, this purgatorial or therapeutic area is not peopled by the Fae. There are no dwarves or elves or swan maidens walking around in it, only human beings and such other creatures (cats, dogs, cows, horses, birds, etc.) as they could have seen while they were alive. Nevertheless, such a place can be seen as one aspect of Faerie, in so far as Faerie is an old name for all the Otherworld, and also in so far as the word 'faerie' derives from the word *fatum* meaning 'fate'. And we do get to see where our fate has been leading us when we are in the Otherworld.

The Celts seem to have had similar beliefs. As well as the Celtic paradise called *Tír na nÓg/Hy Brasil* 'the Isle of Apples', there were other more challenging places in which you could find yourself facing various perils and temptations. Afterwards, each person was believed to be reborn in this World. Existence could take many forms, including those of animals and plants, but after enough experience for the gaining of wisdom and integrity, there could eventually be a permanent homecoming to an Otherworldly realm of light and harmony. However, a descent into dishonour and corruption could lead to a sojourn in outer darkness and chaos. This is a simplified version of how our ancestors thought of the Afterlife, but in neither Nordic nor Celtic belief does there seem to have been much in the way of judgment by a stern God. It is rather that each of us goes into the state/place that is of the same nature as our own souls or which our souls have somehow required. In other words, our true state of being is mirrored back to us after death, even more acutely than here in this living World.

Such rites as Barbara's faerie funeral can be done in many ways, drawing from the treasure house of faerie lore and folk traditions. You should feel free to let inspiration take over concerning any rites for the dead because then what you do will be heartfelt and real. There could never be one true way of doing faerie rites, any more than there could be one true poem or just one way to tell any story. Study these things as much as you can and contemplate their inner meaning, and then ask the Faerie Queen or any faerie guide whom you may have to help and inspire you. But remember, we are invoking the Powers who take the dead to the Otherworld and through the processes of their existence when there – and that is all. We are not responsible for the dead person's beliefs or progress or anything like that since the dead have their own autonomy within the greater context of Nature. Besides, I feel that their own spiritual beliefs must be respected, just as I hope that mine will be when I am gone from here.

By the way, at Barbara's more official Christian funeral, Ashley was one of the pall-bearers. He says that after the ceremony, the spirit of a young girl preceded the coffin out of the church. We wondered if the Faerie realm had sent one of their own to be a representative. Of course, there are other explanations for such an apparition, but this was the one that occurred to us.

114

CHAPTER NINE

BACK AND FORTH
BETWEEN THE WORLDS

Years ago, I knew a young Englishman who said that in a previous life during the Second World War, he had been a German. Even as a little boy he had believed this about himself. When he was playing at toy soldiers with the other children, he always insisted that the German side was his own. They were his people. For a little English boy in the 1960s, this may have been quite a difficult thing to say. You simply did not express an allegiance with those who had fought on the German side; not in those days, not in England. In fact, he was not saying that he sympathized with Nazi ideas; as a small boy, he did not even know what those had been. He merely claimed that he had fought with the Germans during the War and had himself been German.

People do not usually reincarnate quite randomly in a new place, nor do we pick out the country we fancy for our next life as though choosing a holiday destination from a brochure. Most of us are reborn among people we already know in a country with which we already have past-life connections. This is because links of love or unresolved issues, or both, will draw us back, and most of us do prefer it that way. However, there can be times when a life among strangers in a strange land can offer particular circumstances that suit the incarnating soul more. The new place may present different challenges and opportunities, in terms of personal evolution or of our goals in the service of life. So perhaps the little boy who had been German had strong reasons for choosing a life in England. But there is another explanation.

As we know, some people are earthbound between their lives. In his book *Exploring Reincarnation* Hans TenDam tells us that some living people state, under hypnosis, that they missed the chance to go fully into the Otherworld after their last death. They simply missed their way and wandered about in a realm between this and the Otherworld – somewhere between. They were ghosts, in fact, but not malevolent ones – only confused and lost. No one from Faerie came to rescue them; no one among the living noticed their plight.

This kind of thing is said to be more likely when someone dies very suddenly, as may happen during a war. In time, such people may resolve the situation for themselves by noticing a pregnant woman in the vicinity and, as it were, moving in. This may be quite easy and, it is said, can even be done when a child has already been born. This is because some newborns and some young children are quite ambivalent about being back here in this World. (Well, let's face it: this can be a heartbreaking, gruelling place if you are unlucky.) Offered the chance to swap places with another soul, they may gladly take that chance, reckoning that they know their way back to Faerie – after all, they have just come from there so it cannot be too difficult to find. Or so the theory goes. If this is true, it shows the after-death state to be more anarchic than we might have thought or have been taught. At any rate, between the Worlds, there seems to be a state where choice and change are less carefully planned and more spontaneous.

That young man I mentioned was born in the south of England, in an area where many German pilots had been shot down. And so perhaps he did the only thing that seemed possible to him or which seemed desirable. This is only conjecture, it might not be true. But I am raising it to illustrate that there are a great many possible outcomes when someone dies. For example, he could have been helped by a living psychic person if he had been noticed. (There are some witches and spiritualists and other psychics who specialize in helping the earthbound dead to go through to the Otherworld.) As it was, my imagined dead airman was likely to have been very frightened, disoriented, young and a long way from home. And he might not have wanted to go back to Germany; might not have been a Nazi himself; might have been a conscripted pilot – we cannot know.

This plight could as easily have befallen a British airman or soldier killed in a foreign land. However, I imagine the dead Briton being more likely to make for a Channel port and try to get home. The idea would come naturally because of living on an island. And actually, the First World War poet Edward Thomas may have implied this in his poem 'Roads'. (Thomas died in France in 1917.)

Now all roads lead to France
and heavy is the tread
of the living; but the dead
returning lightly dance.

Whatever the road bring
to me or take from me,

they keep me company
with their pattering,

crowding the solitude
of the loops over the downs,
hushing the roar of towns
and their brief multitude.

I mention this to illustrate that not every ghost is spiteful.
In the case I have just described, my imagined dead airman
is likely to have been in a pitiable state. I think of him
wandering in the fields and lanes of post-war England, a
wraith, and very bewildered. Then he found a way to live
a human life all over again.

In her books about death and the dying, Elizabeth
Kuhbler-Ross describes the entrance to the Otherworld as
a tunnel filled with golden light. It seems some people do
not manage to find it or any other entrance. They do not
find the Faerie Boatman, either. Or they do find something, but are afraid, not recognizing it for what it is.

Our blessings and prayers for the newly dead may be
more necessary than most of us realize. They may turn the
fate of someone lost between Worlds, enabling them to
find their way through to where there is rest and healing
in the Otherworld. Or – and this is more likely – enabling
Otherworldly rescuers to find them. They then have a
better chance to reincarnate according to inner or spiritual
purposes.

We, the living, can call out to those who may help to
bring the disoriented dead home from their wanderings.
As I have said, I would, myself, call on the Faerie King or
the Swan Maidens. These last, who can take the form of
swans, ravens or crows as well as of women, are said not
only to bring the dead to the Otherworld, but especially to

care for those who have died in battle. If I were a Christian, I might call out to guiding angels. Those of other faiths would call to whomsoever their own tradition recommends for this situation.

Remember, everything after death is as varied as it is in life, as full of Mystery and possibilities. Just as when we are born, at death there are no guarantees. This can mean that the about-to-be-born can be faced with challenges. For a pregnant woman (or father-to-be) the best thing to do about this is just what it always traditionally was: ask the Great Mother (the Source) to keep the little soul safe at all times. And speak to the unborn child inside your heart, offering love and care – so strengthening that child's courage.

As to the earthbound dead, we can call to the Fae or to Elves of Light (angels) to come to the rescue – and this is a job that the fey-spirited person can do easily. Being especially sensitive to a discarnate presence and able to call for help with informal ease makes us quite good at this. The exceptions to these cases would be when there is a bad spirit with a cruel disposition. If this is the case – and you will know it is because you will sense it in the atmosphere – then it is best to get away from the haunted place as soon as you can. Later on, from a much safer place (such as your own home or a tranquil garden or quiet hill-top), you can call on the Faerie King (inside your mind as when saying a prayer) and ask for the Fae to intervene. In cases where the earthbound soul seems evasive as well as malevolent, you may need to find a trained exorcist. Each one of us needs to recognize when we may be out of our depth; we must then call in someone of wider knowledge and specialist skills. A fey person who is an exorcist is in a strong position, of course. I myself am not one: in spite of almost forty years as a Fay, hedge witch and psychic counsellor, I have never been drawn to exorcism.

A Fay, in case you are wondering, is a fey person who casts spells. The word 'fay' derives from the Latin *fatum* meaning 'fate'. This is the root of the French *fée* and the English word 'faerie'. A Fay is a person who can weave fate by the use of enchantments. A Fay chants or sings or speaks words for a magical purpose, as do witches and Druidic bards. All this makes a lot more sense when you know that the Proto-Indo European word *bha* is the origin of the Latin *fatum* and our English word 'fate', and also means 'speech', 'announcement' and 'prophecy' as well as 'enchantment'.

It is important to stay within the area of our own magical capabilities, but equally important to value the simple psychic help anyone can give. For those needing assistance on their journey to or from the Otherworld – the dead and the unborn children – our prayers and blessings and requests for intervention can tip the scales and bring a good outcome – whoever we are. To demonstrate the importance of such blessings, here is an excerpt from my diary in which I have written down a conversation I had with my faerie familiar one day in autumn 2015.

This is a fine September morning with a light mist. It is said in folklore that faeries like misty weather and travel around in it. That is very interesting as it links with the old idea from traditional witchcraft that paths connecting this and the Otherworld can be made by sprinkling water along the ground. I don't know for how far. Anyway, it seems a good day to invoke my familiar, the elven man, in spite of the fact that he's always come to me in any weather. I do it by calling his name three times within my own mind and also by mentioning symbols and themes which are connected with him and his kind. Thus:

'By white gull feather, by clouds that drift like woodsmoke from autumn bonfires, by mist, by all that appears and yet disappears, by all the hidden laws of travel between the Worlds, I call to you, my kindly familiar.'

He responds at once and then we have a conversation that I have recorded while it was happening, writing it all down in a rough scrawl. It is, of course, taking place in the language of elves. We are speaking Elvish. That is to say, our ideas and thoughts are travelling back and forth between the Worlds in a form that is beyond words. Meanwhile, my own mind is supplying an instant translation into English while his, equally swiftly, is giving a translation into his own faerie language. We each provide the words that are needed and in our own idiom, but the wordless language of spirit remains the common tongue.

RAE What would you most like to say to those in my World, the living World? I've been asked to be a medium for things like that – well, haven't I? So what would the Fae – and especially elves of your kind – most like to say to whoever would listen amongst living humans?

ELF What should I say to a species that has done more wrong and yet more kindly deeds than any other? Living humans have such ugly, twisted dreams. And yet there are those among you who dream with beauty and harmony. And both types of dream are lived out! Humans have been this way all through the Ages. We who live where I dwell in the Otherworld would say this – if we thought anyone was really listening. Take this from our lips and hearts. Do not believe your species could continue to exist for the time of an egg in a pan to boil if not being given your best chance by ancestral blessings.

RAE   Whatever can you mean?

ELF   Make this a clear thing for people to hear in your own World. Put it into your book. All beings have forebears and the forebears want life, abundant life for their descendants – their children, grandchildren, great- and great-great-grandchildren, and on and on through future years. Most living people as well as the dead want that. Even those who do not have children want it for future generations. This is what the dead want. Even though people now pay scant attention to the memory of the dead, have turned away from the shrines to the ancestors long since, all down the stone-cold and stone-deaf centuries, forebears have been blessing living people because enough living people remained who still spoke to them in their hearts and so maintained the connection. Living people should honour their forebears because they passed on life and knowledge. They passed on love of the land's beauty and they bequeathed their natural wisdom. They knew just where to build roads and houses with respect for the land's contours and all its waterways. They knew of drainage for lowlands – rhynes and dykes and ditches to prevent flooding. They knew the ways of the creatures and plants. Their landscapes held meaning. Not long ago, people knew where their grandparents had gone out courting. And which local lanes or buildings were haunted. And which years had given the best apple harvest and where two fishermen had washed up ashore alive when their boat had sunk. And they also knew loss and ill-health and bitterness, food shortages and war and injustice. And so they bless their descendants with survival and with fertile land and with good fortune, knowing just how much such blessings are needed. All of this helps to keep all life in being. It helps far more than the living realize.

RAE   Wait! Just a minute! Those who caused wars and those who were unjust, cruel and brutal were also ancestors. What about them? Do they not also bless their own kin? And do they not bless their own psychological descendants, those of today's people who are equally unscrupulous? If so, then they may not be helping to keep the World in existence, but be doing the opposite. Aren't they blessing today's plunderers and robber barons and all who lay waste to the land for the sake of their own profit?

ELF   Not at all! Because they are not of sound understanding that your World continues without them, they do not bless anyone living when not themselves alive anymore. Besides, those who live without care and consideration for others or for the land do not bless anyone except perhaps their own children, and then only during their own lifetime. This type of human cannot imagine the living World going on without them; they only imagine it with themselves in it. They have no feeling that life has a point to it if they are not a living part of it. It is not simply that they don't care, not even about their own children. It is just that they have minds so blinkered

123

ıt the World after their own future death is
ıt something they can believe in. It is not real
them. This is the most extreme kind of solip-
sm. After they die they have still these same
attitudes and so they cannot conceive of the
living, and so they don't bless them. Anyway, the
most corrupt among them cannot survive death
as the individuals they have been. Their souls are
terminally sick and so die along with the body
and become psychic compost. Only their spirits
survive and these have a new start as a new being
– no connection and no continuity with what
they were before, which no longer exists.

RAE   I expect we have all had some ancestors who
were like that. Well, bound to have had!

ELF   Many have had some very hard-hearted ancestors, and yet themselves been bright and loving.
These people are blessed by their more kindly
forebears and by their ancestors of soul.

RAE   What are the 'ancestors of soul'?

ELF   They are often called 'ancestors of spirit' rather
then ancestors of soul. They are those from
whom your soul has inherited its particular
orientation in inner things. Your personal spirituality or spiritual tone comes from these. This
has nothing to do with religion and applies just
as much to those your World calls the
Humanists. And actually, from our Faerie point
of view, the Humanists are often very developed
spiritually. They are often honest people. They
have integrity. They can be sensitive to beauty
and they do often care about other life forms
and the health of the land. They have healthy
souls and are not afraid of sensuality. We call this

'harmony' in our World. It is, to us, what spiritual progress is all about. Not all Humanists are like that, but a lot of them are. Anyway, ancestors of soul have bequeathed to these and to many others their ideas and beliefs, their songs and stories, their poems and pictures and traditions. Most of them are not related to you by blood. And they can be of any race and from any land on Earth. Some of them may never have lived in your World at all, but are of Faerie. And these all bless you because they feel that they have an inner kinship.

RAE   Would you tell me more, please, about faerie spirituality?

ELF   Yes – to the Fae, being spiritual means acknowledging spirit in all things. We are what your World calls 'animistic'. This means knowing deep in your heart that all are your kin, all beings of all species, all the creatures and plants and even the stones beneath your feet. This is because all are born of the same Great Mother of All Life, She who is formless and yet can take any form. This kind of spirituality means being strong in truth and yet wild and free like a tree or a river. It means you live with respect for the needs of all species. We of the Fae experience ourselves as a part of all Nature. We do not think we are separate from Nature and so this comes easily and so does natural magic. We do not have a religion at all. Humans have lots of religions and also spirituality, but these are not always hand in hand.

RAE   Thank you – they certainly are not. But can we go back to where you began? You were saying that all the living depend on ancestral blessings? **ELF** Yes, but these are beginning to decrease because the living do not honour the dead as much as they used to. They do not remember to bless their dead parents and grandparents and all kindly forebears. They do not even talk to them inside their hearts very much. It is as though they believe that death is not a real part of life, not inevitable, and that, therefore, the dead must be somehow at fault and best forgotten. They do not seem to understand that their griefs and struggles are very like the ones their ancestors knew, in spite of changes in belief and opportunities and tools. So they do not honour their forebears. Worst of all, many of them do not think that the dead exist except, possibly, as something dangerous.

If the living do not remember to bless their dead, then important links are broken between the generations and between the Worlds. And then the living can no longer see that they are fulfilling themes and purposes – such as the gaining of knowledge or wisdom, or the development of skills – that are much longer-lasting than their own short lives. And the broken links between the dead and the living can mean broken lives. For when the dead are not remembered, they also start to forget the living eventually. And then such blessings as could have made a crucial difference are not bestowed. And also the living no longer have such a sense of belonging in your World. For all their brash feeling that they alone matter, they do not feel they have roots; their souls are not always rooted in deeply enough to gain inner strength.

RAE   But the animals and plants don't acknowledge their ancestors, nor do they seek blessings from them, and they get on fine. So why should we need this?

ELF   The animals and plants remember within their bodies and instincts about connections with aspects of Nature that gave their forebears a home and will house their descendants. They do not deny their own place within cycles of life that are larger than they are because they lack any conscious awareness about that subject. And so they do not have humanity's conscious ability to disremember. Humankind must make a conscious decision to remember and to well-wish their forebears and their descendants. For that is what blessing means. It is well-wishing. And this should include blessings for the non-human ancestors, too: those of the plants and creatures whose bones and essences lie in the land; plants and creatures who were all part of the biosphere and made the lives of the ancestors possible. Plants and creatures who fed or clothed or warmed or taught or companioned the human ancestors must be well-wished, especially. To bless the ancestors of place and soul as well as of family increases a sense of belonging for living humans and also a sense of responsibility to future generations. And it gains loving attention from those in the Realm of Soul – in Faerie.

At this point, my faerie familiar paused.

ELF   I have just one real message: humankind must
       stop all this disremembering and disrespect for
       their forebears *and* their descendants; people
       must bless those of goodwill who lived before
       and also those who will live in the future. This
       has nothing to do with patriotism or family
       pride and it never leads to a war. For a true
       blessing of the forebears soon deepens into a
       knowing that we are all, if we reach far enough
       back in time, kin to one another, children of one
       Great Mother-Father Spirit, First Cause of All
       Life. Or, to put it another way, children of Earth
       and starfire. That is all I have to say.

RAE   What more could be said? Except . . . I would
       still like to know why you claim the living could
       not go on for longer than it takes an egg to boil
       in a pan without the blessing of our forebears.
       Why should it matter so acutely as you seem to
       say it does?

ELF   Because otherwise there would be no way to heal
       the great rift between humanity's self-serving
       behaviour and the true needs of all the rest of the
       natural world. Too many of today's humans have
       become as the type of ancestor who cannot bless
       their own descendants because they cannot imag-
       ine the World would be here or would matter if
       they were dead. And they cannot understand
       their dependency on land and air and water and
       other species. They think of Nature as a back-
       drop or as something to use. They plunder the
       Earth for trivial objects such as furniture they
       don't need and for strange playthings. They
       destroy other species. They poison the seas. They
       jeopardize the future of all life on Earth with

their wars and greed. From the Faerie perspective, humans are a species running amok. And yet their extraordinary intelligence, creativity and awareness make them beloved of Mother Earth – just as an unusually gifted but unbalanced adolescent will be loved by a human mother, however much he makes her suffer. Humans must care about how much their behaviour affects other generations and other species. Too many of them do not acknowledge the needs of anything but humanity, and then only those who are living now. To be so isolated within the shell of their own being and yet so ingenious about what they make, that is to be in danger and to be dangerous. That is why the living depend on the love of the ancestors more than ever.

RAE I see.

ELF My message is now given. Now I will wing above the sea in the Otherworld and cry the cry of a gull. And afterwards I will fly to the land and descend to a clearing within a wood and there shift my shape into that of a man in a feather cloak. Next, I will light a fire and sit by it and I will think of your World and be glad I'm not there! Then I may become a drift of mist for the restfulness of it. And after that, I will maybe join in a dance at the edge of the sea. I will dance in starlight while white foam curves around stone and shell and the waters tell tales of faerie magic and bells ring from under the waves.

RAE Can I go there with you?

ELF Not today. You have many things still to do in the living World and that is where, in your heart, you still desire to be.

So ends my diary entry – for now. Dear reader, if you, too, speak with the Fae, you may not hear such bleak, angry words as those I have just shared. Indeed, this same familiar may speak more gently and more positively of human beings on another occasion. But faerie anger about human destruction of the environment is widespread. And his message is really very simple. It comes down to this: the World in which humans can survive is held in existence by the care of the ancestors for the living . . . and by the care of the living for their own offspring, or other peoples', or for the land itself – by love, in fact. His anger springs from the fact that he does not think we yet love enough.

CHAPTER TEN

MRS ELDRIDGE REFLECTS

Mrs Eldridge stands in her garden enjoying the autumn sunshine. She hears crows cawing as they fly overhead. Her mind shifts in response to them. Now she is sensing the links between these birds and herself, the psychic threads that bind her to wild flight and the tops of trees and to wind currents and light and to all that live in the wide sky. They bind her, also, to the Otherworld where these birds will eventually fly. She herself is walking to the Otherworld throughout her human life for this is the fate of all creatures; she knows this. From time to time, Mrs Eldridge has walked right into the Otherworld and then walked back out while still alive, enriched by her meeting there with the Faerie Queen or a faerie familiar. But she knows that one day she will have walked far enough and then her body will fall like a small bird in a harsh winter while her soul will just walk on to the Otherworld and not come out.

In her body, she dreads that moment, as do all living creatures. Besides, there are people and places she will miss. And yet, in her soul, she looks forward to that last walk across the boundary between this World and the Other. She knows well enough how to find her way. (People like Mrs Eldridge are never earthbound.) She will be going home.

Today, in this World, she has things to do. She floats a small boat on her garden pond. She has filled its tiny hold with minute portions of food and herbal medicines and little blankets. She knows that just as surely as her boat has a reflection in the pool, its faerie counterpart sets off in Otherworldly waters. She casts a heartfelt spell that the faerie boat shall reach a distant shore, the faerie coast of – (here she names a country within this World). And that it shall be the size of a large human ship. (Here she places an acorn in the water to encourage magically the process of enlargement.) And bring help to those who need it in that distant land – in our own World.

She works in the realm of Soul using image and symbol, as our dreams do, knowing that the reflections fly back and forth between World and World. Mrs Eldridge concludes with the following lines:

> As in Faerie, so in the living World.
> From the land where I dwell, a ship
> sets off and arrives safely.
> It brings great help to those who most need it.
> In the name of the Great Mother,
> the Queen of All Fate, so may this be.

Knowing just how easily a spell may go awry, she has earlier described the plight of the people to whom she wishes help to be given. And she has stated exactly what kind of help this is going to be. It is important to be this precise when working magic: an unfocused spell will bring a vague, or even irrelevant, result. (Mrs Eldridge has

132

learned this the hard way in her youth.)

The tiny boat sets off. Now, in a distant country, suffering people will receive a bit more help than they have before. Mrs Eldridge does magic of this kind rather a lot. Such spells are easy for her and for Lizzie and Johnnie and all their fey friends. But they do come at a price for those who cast them. This is because our inner selves and also our lives are altered – for good or ill – by any magic we do, even when it is for others. 'Best to be on your guard then and try to do no harm – since in doing it, you harm your own self.' So Mrs Eldridge believes, and she is no fool.

Another more obvious price that may be paid by fey people is that of being misunderstood by more conventional types, as we know. This may lead to being mocked and marginalized or in some way condemned. She knows that in the past witches, wisewomen, cunning men, psychic healers and seers have been executed for what she does. Or even – like Joan of Arc – for simply speaking with faeries. Well, times have changed, for now. There are other threats these days, directed more randomly at many types of human being. This is an insane World that we live in, Mrs Eldridge reckons.

'What can have driven human beings quite this mad?' she wonders. 'Is it the fear of death? Or is it the huge distance between what their souls know and what their minds believe? Or is it that any one of us, if pushed far enough, might do something terrible? And that the weakest or the least healthily nourished souls break soonest?'

She thinks so. She thinks this last idea is the true answer, and sighs. There seems to be no alternative to the long trudge towards psychological and spiritual evolution for every one of us – that long journey in and out of the Otherworld in life after life – for developing greater love and some kind of wisdom. 'At least,' she says to herself, 'we can ask for faerie advice along the way.'

The writer Orion Foxwood in his book *The Faery Teachings* tells us that both faeriekind and humankind are the offspring of one elder race; that, in fact, faeries and humans are close cousins as species, but have developed on different lines. Now, however, faeriekind has withdrawn to the Otherworld because the psychic and physical atmosphere created by human activities is too dense. These are the legends. (Interestingly, I have noticed that many of today's fey humans are also particularly sensitive to unpleasant atmospheres and airborne pollution.)

A Christian legend (or myth) tells us that faeriekind once came to Earth from the stars as fallen angels. The Reverend Robert Kirk, a minister of the Scottish Church in the late seventeenth century, had more detailed information. He tells us, in his book *The Secret Commonwealth of Elves, Fauns and Fairies*:

'These siths or fairies . . . are said to be of a middle nature betwixt man and angel, as were demons of old, of intelligent studious spirits and light changeable bodies (like those called astral) somewhat of the nature of a condensed cloud and best seen in twilight.'

He had also learned that the faeries/fairies do not present a misty intangible appearance when seen within their own World (rather than in ours). In their own realm, says Robert Kirk:

'Their apparel and speech is like that of the people under whose country they live' – by which he means within a subtle dimension of the land rather than under it literally as cave dwellers might be – '. . . so they are seen to wear plaids and variegated garments in the Highlands of Scotland and *suanochs*, [garments made from tartan] therefore in Ireland. . . . Their women are said to spin very fine, to dye, to tissue, and embroider: but whether it is a manual operation of substantial refined stuffs with apt and solid instruments, or only curious cobwebs, impalpable rainbows, and a fantastic imitation of the actions of more terrestrial mortals . . . I leave to conjecture as I found it.'

The Fae themselves most probably laugh at our attempts to categorize them. Nature spirits? Gods and Goddesses of Earth and the stars? Guides and helpers of the dead? A folk memory of former races no longer living in our World? We cannot generalize for there are all these and more within the Otherworld. After all, there are many types and species and orders of being within Faerie (including faerie plants and creatures). Crucially, the Fae embrace paradox. It is no trouble to them to explain that they are both divine and savage, have lived human lives in some cases even though they are not human, and that they are of starfire and yet very much of the nature of Earth. Some of them mediate the power of a constellation of stars – an example is Gwyn ap Nudd, who is believed by some to be linked with Orion – and yet live within or close to the abode of the dead *within the land*. Their bodies can appear to us to be made out of light or mist and yet in their own World they are as solid as you or I.

In fact, our human distinctions can often seem foolish to them. And it has been pointed out by Orion Foxwood in his first-rate books about faerie lore that we are the ones who can appear to be made out of mist or light – for that is how our souls can look to those in the Otherworld while we are still living. From their point of view, it is we who can seem to 'haunt' the Otherworld. The Reverend Robert Kirk described these apparitions of the living, calling them 'co-walkers'. He meant that our souls are within Nature's Otherworld, even while we still live. (This may be easier to understand when we remember that the Otherworld is not somewhere cut off from here, but a parallel dimension of

our World and, of course, vice versa.) Even an object such
as a boat can have, if not a soul, then something compara-
ble. Perhaps it is ensouled because of the way many
humans relate to it as a boat, as though the boat were
sentient: ensouled, in fact, by a part of the psyche of each
human being who has constructed it, worked with it, sailed
in it – who knows? Yet somehow I feel that Nature herself
ensouls everything, even at the level of raw materials or
very primal things. Naturally, these are not anything like
human souls, but are impersonal as clouds or moonbeams.
At any rate, some kind of counterpart of object as well as
creature does definitely exist in the realm of Faerie. 'Co-
walkers' of objects within our living World can certainly
appear within that Otherworldly place that is nearest to
our own, even if not in the further and deeper reaches of
Faerie (where no one amongst the Fae would want them or
allow them to roam). It is this belief upon which Mrs
Eldridge bases her magic, as do many witches and other
magical workers. However, she knows that the Faerie
counterpart of any object (or person) may not look like
their appearance in our World. Instead, it will express their
true psychic state. For example, a self-absorbed soul may
appear to be deaf or blind in the Otherworld. This would
be because they are oblivious to a great deal they hear or
see within the living World. On the other hand, in the
living World, people who are deaf or blind physically may
be so for a number of organic, dietary or environmental
reasons, not necessarily connected with any psychic or
inner factors of their own choosing. As ever, these things
may be paradoxical, fluid and connected with the common
lot of humanity, or just with life on Earth.

My faerie teacher tells me that the Fae just cannot
understand the human desire to put things into categories,
boxes, computer programs within their heads, with every-

thing defined in one way only and that definition meant to be final. To them, we are all multi-dimensional beings with bodies, souls and spirits that can shift shape as we move through time. Besides, she says, we are not as separate and distinct as we think we are. Each one of us is a part of the locality within which we dwell, our souls an expression of some aspect of that region's soul (as our bodies and spirits are expressions of the place and the time that we live in). Ultimately, we are each expressions, parts, aspects of the Earth. And beyond even that, we are differing expressions of one Great Being that is the Spirit that runs in all things that exist, in all galaxies and all dimensions.

It seems to be true, as the Reverend Kirk said, that the Fae have 'no discernible religion'. (My familiar spirit has confirmed this.) Their grasp of reality is poetic and fluid and spiritual rather than religious. They also lack the sharp focus of present-day human rationality, but are inclusive and transrational. Many fey people think similarly. To both the Fae and the fey, there is nothing so stupid as reductionism. They see it as rather like saying that just because you know, scientifically, how a concert is broadcast that therefore music does not exist because it is 'nothing but' airwaves, radio signals and so forth.

Mrs Eldridge has no truck with anything reductionist or fundamentalist. Her understanding is many-faceted and so her soul is free. Now she stares and stares into the bright mirror of her garden pond. She no longer sees an Otherworldly ship, for that spell is done. Instead, she sees the face of an elven teacher, he whose slanting eyes are grey but flecked with silver.

'It is time for me to answer your earlier question,' he says. 'What are you living humans really doing in your World – why are you there? Well, for one thing, we of the

Otherworld learn much by the experience of humans – and other species. Fae such as myself learn from human insights and memories. We often glean these things from those who have died. Many come into the Otherworld with their souls full of their impressions of your World's beauty and of all that they have ever loved. And yet they may have been tried nearly beyond endurance while they were alive. Their souls can be very strong because they've been nourished by beauty and love and by their own quest for truth. They may have gained both strength and wisdom. That wisdom will have been distilled from many experiences of ugliness as well as of beauty, and of cruelty as well as love and of lies, as well as of truth.

'Humans have a hard part to play. They are currently immersed in harsh experience and in much suffering. And rather a lot of it stems from the ruthlessness of their own kind. As a species, they fell from innocence long ago. And they have created a river of blood by their wars and their many murders. But such wisdom as they are attaining through their plight is also of help to us. It is gained by human effort, but it helps us, too!'

'But many of your kind are already so much wiser than we are!' Mrs Eldridge cries.

'I have learned from you and from others like you,' insists the elven man. 'I have first learned as our race learns in our own World. But then you and I have *exchanged* knowledge. In this way and in many others the Great Spirit that runs through all things acquires experience and moves towards an ever-increasing wisdom.'

Mrs Eldridge ponders this revelation. There is Mystery at the heart of it even though it seems to her to be straight-forward.

Mirrors, reflections, exchanges, conjoinings; and opposites as alike and yet unlike as the dawn and dusk. She knows her conscious mind will never grasp all there is to know about the Otherworld, or even this one or why we live in them. But there are portals between the Worlds and each somehow completes the other. (Let that be enough – for today, anyway?) But she wants to go on learning and she feels privileged to explore all this.

Where are we going, eventually?

Mrs Eldridge sings her star chant while she waters the garden.

Under the stars, a soul
who has parted from both body and hearth
looks up and sees the white wings
of a great swan.

It comes down beside her onto bleak ground.
Astride the feathered back she is borne up
for she weighs no more than a loving heart.
There is ice hanging in the air and the ice rings.
And the swan's neck is ringed by a gold chain.
And it seems that all that was warm land has passed.

Now there is nowhere to go but into the north
and on and on and on through the dark north
until dark gives way to an arc of rainbow
somewhere beyond the back of the north wind
in the light of stars.

This is her soul's choice and her heart's compass.
And then the white swan
who has always known
and has come to fetch her back to her rightful home
will set her down gently in light and beauty.

So let it be for each one of us.
However long the way through life after life,
so let it be for each one of us.

Now Mrs Eldridge looks forward to the evening. She will sit by the fire with a glass of beer and watch a good film. She will forget for a while the challenges of her own fey life. In spite of the state of this World, she does feel hope and faith deep within. 'We will get there eventually,' she thinks. 'Humans will change and grow and evolve in spirit and achieve harmony – if not in this World, then in the Other and in some other way. For we are not separate and lost. Our souls are a part of the Great Soul of Nature. Our spirits are each an aspect of one Great Spirit. We are part of All. We can never be apart from the rest – we are part of it.'

She settles down with her cat.

Outside, Lizzie and Johnnie walk hand in hand down by the river. The hobgoblin has made his way home by now and the crows are resting.

Night falls again on the Island of Britain, covering Cornwall, England, Wales, the Isle of Man, Scotland and all smaller islands and the surrounding seas. And behind every mundane face of hill or valley in town or country, the old faerie magic is awake and active.

BIBLIOGRAPHY

Collins, Andrew, *The Cygnus Mystery*, Watkins Publishing, 2006

Dathen, Jon, *Somerset Faeries and Pixies: Exploring Their Hidden World*, Capall Bann, 2010

Devereux, Paul, *Haunted Land*, Piatkus, 2001

Evans-Wentz, W.Y., *The Fairy Faith in Celtic Countries*, Citadel Press, 1990

Foxwood, Orion, *The Faery Teachings*, R.J. Stewart Books, 2008

Franklin, Anna, *The Illustrated Encyclopaedia of Fairies*, Vega, 2002

Grigsby, John, *Warriors of the Wasteland*, Watkins Publishing, 2003

Kirk, Robert, *The Secret Commonwealth of Elves, Fauns and Fairies*, Dover Publications, 2008

Saleem, Ramses, *The Egyptian Book of Life*: A True Translation of the Papyrus of Enhai and the Papyrus of Hunefer: 'The Egyptian Book of the Dead', Watkins Publishing, 2004

Sikes, Wirt, *British Goblins: Welsh Folklore, Fairy Mythology, Legends and Traditions*, Sampson Low, 1880

Stewart, R.J., *The Living World of Faery*, Mercury Publishing, 1995

TenDam, Hans, *Exploring Reincarnation*, Penguin Books, 1990

Welch, Lynda, *Goddess of the North*, Red Wheel, 2001

SUGGESTED READING

Arrowsmith, Nancy, *Field Guide to the Little People*, Llewellyn Publications, 2009

Artisson, Robin, *The Witching Way of the Hollow Hill*, Pendraig Publishing, 2006

Berg, Wendy, *Red Tree, White Tree: Faeries and Humans in Partnership*, Skylight Press, 2010

Beth, Rae, *Lamp of the Goddess: Lives and Teachings of a Priestess*, previously titled *Reincarnation and the Dark Goddess*, Robert Hale, 1994

Brown, Nimue, *Druidry and the Ancestors*, Moon Books, 2012

Carding, Emily, *Faery Craft: Weaving Connection with the Enchanted Realm*, Llewellyn Publications, 2012

Dale, Cyndi, *Illuminating the Afterlife*, Sounds True, 2008

Durdin-Robertson, Lawrence, *Life in the Next World*, Cesara Publications, 1989

Forest, Danu, *Nature Spirits: Wyrd Lore and Wild Fey Magic*, Wooden Books, 2008

Foxwood, Orion, *The Tree of Enchantment; Ancient Wisdom and Magic Practices of the Faery Tradition*, Red Wheel/Weiser, 2008

Goodwin, Melba, *Ghost Worlds: A Guide to Poltergeists, Portals, Ectomist and Spirit Behaviour*, Llewellyn Publications, 2009

James, Catrin, *Celtic Faery Shamanism: Wisdom of the Otherworld*, Capall Bann, 1999

Knight, Gareth, *The Faery Gates of Avalon*, R.J. Stewart Books, 2008

Kubler-Ross, Elizabeth, *The Wheel of Life: A Memoir of Living and Dying*, Touchstone, 1998

McArthur, Margie, *Faery Healing: the Lore and the Legacy*, New Brighton Books, 2003

Mynne, Hugh, *The Faerie Way*, Llewellyn Publications, 1996

Pennick, Nigel, *The Eldritch World*, Lear Books, 2006

Stewart, R.J., *The Well of Light: from Faery Healing to Earth Healing*, Muse Press, 2004

Rae's website
www.raebeth.com

Other books by Rae Beth:

The Hedge Witch
The Hedge Witch's Way
Lamp of the Goddess: Lives and Teachings of a Priestess
Spellcraft for Hedge Witches: A Guide to Healing Our Lives
The Green Hedge Witch: A Guide to Wild Magic